AF377723

General Knowledge Olympiad

Class 06

A must have book for all
Olympiads & Talent Search Exams...

by
Nandini Sharma

BLOOM CAP
Bloom Cap Edu Ventures Pvt. Ltd.

Bloom Cap Edu Ventures Pvt. Ltd.

© **Publisher**

No part of this publication may be re-produced, stored in a retrieval system or by any means, electronic, mechanical, photocopying, recording, scanning, web or otherwise without the written permission of the publisher. Publisher has obtained all the information in this book from the sources believed to be reliable and true. However, Publisher or its editors or authors or illustrators don't take any responsibility for the absolute accuracy of any information published and the damage or loss suffered thereupon.

All disputes subject to Delhi jurisdiction only.

Administrative & Production Office

'Ramchhaya' 4577/15, Agarwal Road, Darya Ganj, New Delhi -110002
Tele: 011- 47630600, 43518550

ISBN : 978-93-25519-45-9

PRICE : ₹100.00

PO No : TXT-XX-XXXXXXX-X-XX

For further information about the books log on to
www.bloomcap.org

Follow us on   

Preface

"Future belongs to those Who prepares for it today"

School Olympiads are National & International level competitions conducted by different Government, Non-Government & Educational Organisations with the purpose of making the children ready to face competitive exams. The challenging Questions asked in Olympiads motivate them to learn more & more and bring out the best result with improved academic performance. The Awards & Scholarship offered by Olympiads motivate children to aspire & strive for doing better and emerge out to be the best.

GK Olympiads

GK is the knowledge of every aspect of the human life, which may or may not be the part of routine academic studies but very important for the overall personality development of the students. It is more or less connected with the attentiveness and awareness. There can be different domains of GK like; History, Geography, Polity, Culture, Discovery, Sports, Current Affairs etc.

GK Olympiads help students in understanding the importance of General Knowledge and updations about National & International Affairs in daily life..

'Bloom GK Olympiad Study Book Class 6' is a perfect resource to Study & Practice for Olympiad Exams and other National & State Level Talent Search Exams & Other Competitions.

Some Special Features of Bloom GK Olympiad Study Books are;

- Complete coverage of all the topics related to GK;. History, Geography, Environment, Polity, Science, Culture, Sports, etc.
- Chapterwise Exercises having different types of Objective Questions.
- Olympiad Pattern Practice Sets at the end.

This book is prepared by Expert Panel with the utmost care, still if you have any suggestions regarding its improvement then feel free to contact us at olympiads@bloomcap.org. We will try to inculcate your suggestions in the further editions.

BLOOM CAP

Contents

BLOOM CAP

Ancient History of India

1 Mark Questions

1. Wheel was invented during .... age.
   (a) Paleolithic   (b) Mesolithic
   (c) Neolithic   (d) Chalcolithic

2. Due to an extensive use of metals, the ...... is also known as 'Age of Metals'.
   (a) Paleolithic   (b) Mesolithic
   (c) Neolithic   (d) Chalcolithic

3. Which of the following were the earliest domesticated animals?
   (a) Cow and Bull   (b) Dog and Goat
   (c) Hen and Horse   (d) Ox and Buffalo

4. The first site discovered in the Indus Valley Civilisation was ....
   (a) Harappa   (b) Mohenjo Daro
   (c) Kalibangan   (b) Lothal

5. Harappan civilisation flourished on the banks of river ....
   (a) Indus   (b) Yamuna
   (c) Kaveri   (d) Brahmaputra

6. Which of the following animals were found in the Indus Valley Civilisation?
   (a) Elephant   (b) Rhinoceros
   (c) Tiger   (d) All of these

7. What was the main occupation of the people during Vedic period?
   (a) Agriculture
   (b) Fishing
   (c) Architecture
   (d) Handicraft

8. Vedic literature is also known as ....
   (a) Shruti   (b) Smriti
   (c) Samhita   (d) Vedas

9. Who is the most important God mentioned in Rigveda?
   (a) Indra   (b) Agni
   (c) Yam   (d) Varun

10. The hymns of Rigveda are composed in which of the following language?
    (a) Prakrit   (b) Pali
    (c) Sanskrit   (d) Bodo

11. The Vedic people are generally referred to as the ....
    (a) Brahmans   (b) Aryans
    (c) Dasya   (d) Vaishyas

12. How many states were in Mahajanapadas?
    (a) 15   (b) 16
    (c) 17   (d) 18

13. Alexander was the king of ....
(a) Persia   (b) Athens
(c) Sparta   (d) Macedonia

14. Which one of the following periods is also known as Chalcolithic age?
(a) Old Stone age
(b) New Stone age
(c) Copper age
(d) Iron age

15. In which place Buddha delivered his first Sermon?
(a) Kusinagara   (b) Sarnath
(c) Varanasi   (d) Bodh Gaya

16. Who was the first Tirthankara of Jainism?
(a) Mahavira   (b) Rishabhanath
(c) Parshavnath   (d) None of these

17. Who was the son of Chandragupta Maurya?
(a) Bindusara   (b) Ashoka
(c) Brihadratha   (d) Samudragupta

18. ...... was the capital of Mauryan Empire.
(a) Vaishali   (b) Pataliputra
(c) Girivraja   (d) Shravasti

19. The Kalinga war was fought by ....
(a) Ashoka   (b) Chandragupta
(c) Samudragupta   (d) Bindusara

20. From where the word 'Satyameva Jayate' taken?
(a) Rigveda   (b) Bhagavad Gita
(c) Ramayan   (d) Upanishad

21. Harshacharita was written by ....
(a) Banabhatta   (b) Kalidas
(c) Tulsidas   (d) Abu Fazl

22. ...... was the most famous Kushana ruler.
(a) Harshavardhana
(b) Kanishka
(c) Ashoka
(d) Pushyamitra Shunga

23. Name the Chinese traveller who visited India during the reign of Harshavardhana?
(a) Fa-Hsien   (b) Hiuen-Tsang
(c) I-tsing   (d) None of these

24. The fourth Buddhist Council was convened by ....
(a) Ashoka   (b) Kanishka
(c) Ajatashatru   (d) Kalashoka

2 Marks Questions

25. Which of the following statement is true?
1. Indus Valley Civilisation is the oldest civilisation of India.
2. All the sites of Harappan civilisation are located in India.
3. The Indus Valley Civilisation is also known as the Bronze age civilisation.

Codes
(a) Both 1 and 2
(b) Both 1 and 3
(c) Both 2 and 3
(d) All of the above

26. State T for true and F for false for the given statements.
A. Jainism belives in right faith and right knowledge.
B. Jainism was founded by Lord Mahavira.
C. Mahavira was born in Ahmednagar, Gujarat.

Codes

	A	B	C			A	B	C
(a)	T	T	F		(b)	T	F	T
(c)	F	F	T		(d)	F	T	F

27. State T for true and F for false for the given statements.

A. Mauryan Dynasty was founded by Chandragupta.

B. Bindusara was the son of Chandragupta Maurya.

C. Chanakya was the teacher and the Chief Minister of Chandragupta Maurya.

Codes

	A	B	C
(a)	T	T	T
(b)	F	F	F
(c)	T	F	T
(d)	F	T	F

28. Match the following.

	Events Related to Buddha's Life		Place
A.	Birth	1.	Lumbini
B.	Fourth Council	2.	Kashmir
C.	Enlightenment	3.	Bodhgaya
D.	Death	4.	Kushinagar

Codes

	A	B	C	D		A	B	C	D
(a)	1	2	3	4	(b)	4	3	2	1
(c)	2	1	4	3	(d)	3	4	1	2

29. Match List I with List II.

	List I		List II
A.	Birth of Buddha	1.	Bodh Gaya
B.	Enlightenment	2.	Lumbini
C.	First Sermon	3.	Kushinagar
D.	Death of Buddha	4.	Sarnath

Codes

	A	B	C	D		A	B	C	D
(a)	2	1	3	4	(b)	1	3	4	5
(c)	2	1	4	3	(d)	4	2	1	3

30. Which of the following pair is matched correctly ?

	Empire/ Dynasty	Founder
(a)	Maurya	– Chandragupta Maurya
(b)	Gupta	– Chandragupta-II
(c)	Kanishka	– Ashoka
(d)	All of the above	

Famous Rulers and Kingdoms

1 Mark Questions

1. Qutubuddin Aibak belonged to ....
   (a) Slave dynasty   (b) Khilji dynasty
   (c) Lodhi dynasty   (d) Tughlaq dynasty

2. Iltutmish was the famous ruler of ....
   (a) Delhi sultanate   (b) Golkonda
   (c) Bijapur   (d) Agra

3. The first and only Muslim Lady of Delhi sultanate was ....
   (a) Razia Sultana
   (b) Begum Hazrat Mahal
   (c) Jahanara Begum
   (d) Roshanara Begum

4. Who was the founder of Khilji dynasty?
   (a) Alauddin Khilji
   (b) Jalaluddin Khilji
   (c) Mubarak Khan
   (d) Sikandar Lodhi

5. Ghiyasuddin Tughlaq was the founder of ....
   (a) Lodhi dynasty   (b) Khilji dynasty
   (c) Tughlaq dynasty (d) Slave dynasty

6. The last ruler of Tughlaq dynasty was ....
   (a) Sikandar Lodhi
   (b) Nasiruddin Mohammad Tughlaq
   (c) Md. Bin Tughlaq
   (d) Ghiyasuddin Tughlaq

7. Who was the founder of Lodhi dynasty?
   (a) Bahlol Lodhi
   (b) Sikandar Lodhi
   (c) Ibrahim Lodhi
   (d) Feroz Shah Tughlaq

8. Agra city was founded by which, among the following rulers?
   (a) Sikandar Lodhi
   (b) Feroz Shah Tughlaq
   (c) Mohammad Bin Tughlaq
   (d) Alauddin Khilji

9. Vijayanagara Empire was founded by ....
   (a) Harihara and Bukka
   (b) Saluva Narasimha
   (c) Krishna Deva Raya
   (d) Vira Narasimha

10. Krishan Deva Raya was the ruler of which dynasty?
(a) Tuluva dynasty   (b) Sangama dynasty
(c) Chola dynasty   (d) Pallava dynasty

11. The Battle of Haldighati was won by which king?
(a) Maharana Pratap
(b) Akbar
(c) Prithviraj Chauhan
(d) Shivaji

12. Who among the following laid the foundation of Mughal Empire in 1526?
(a) Aurangzeb   (b) Shah Jahan
(b) Jahangir   (d) Babur

13. Tansen was a great musician during the reign of ....
(a) Babur   (b) Akbar
(c) Shah Jahan   (d) Aurangzeb

14. Which among the following Mughal rulers was known as Zinda Pir?
(a) Jahangir
(b) Humayun
(c) Bahadur Shah Zafar
(d) Aurangzeb

15. Who was the founder of Bahmani Kingdom?
(a) Alauddin Hasan Bahman Shah
(b) Ahmad Shah Abdali
(c) Ibrahim Adil Shah
(d) Bukka

16. Muhammad Bin Tughlaq shifted his capital from Delhi to which city?
(a) Mumbai
(b) Devagiri
(c) Kannauj
(d) Kalikata

17. Which Mughal Emperor was defeated by Sher Shah Suri?
(a) Babur   (b) Humayun
(c) Jahangir   (d) Akbar

18. Mughal Emperor Humayun was succeeded by ....
(a) Akbar   (b) Aurangzeb
(b) Humayun   (d) Jahangir

19. The last ruler of Mughal Empire was ....
(a) Aurangzeb
(b) Shah Jahan
(c) Bahadur Shah Zafar
(d) Bahadur Shah II

20. Who was the founder of Maratha Empire?
(a) Shahu
(b) Shivaji
(c) Rajaram
(d) Balaji Vishwanath

21. Maratha Kingdom was founded by Shivaji during the reign of ....
(a) Mohammad Bin Tughlaq
(b) Akbar
(c) Shah Jahan
(d) Aurangzeb

22. Who became the ruler of Marathas after the death of Shivaji?
(a) Rajaram   (b) Tarabai
(c) Sambhaji   (d) Shahuji

23. The Maratha ruler popularly known as 'Nana Saheb' was ....
(a) Balaji Vishwanath
(b) Baji Rao I
(c) Balaji Baji Rao
(d) Rajaram

2 Marks Questions

24. Which of the following 'Ruler-Dynasty' is not correctly matched?

  (a)   Iltutmish   — Slave Dynasty

  (b)   Alauddin Khilji   — Sayyid Dynasty

  (c)   Feroz Shah Tughlaq   — Tughlaq Dynasty

  (d)   Ibrahim Lodhi   — Lodhi Dynasty

25. Which of the given statements is/are true?

1. Nadir Shah invaded Delhi during Mughal Empire and took away the Kohinoor diamond.
2. Bairam Khan was the commander of Akbar when he ascended the throne.

Codes

(a) Only 1   (b) Only 2

(c) Both 1 and 2   (d) None of these

26. State T for true and F for false for the given statements.

A. Iltutmish completed the construction of Qutub Minar.

B. Razia Sultana was the daughter of Iltutmish.

C. Akbar was the founder of Mughal dynasty in India.

Codes

	A	B	C			A	B	C
(a)	T	T	F		(b)	T	F	T
(c)	F	T	T		(d)	F	F	T

27. Which one of the following pairs (of dynasties and their founders) is not correctly matched?

	Dynasty	Founder
(a)	Slave Dynasty	— Balban
(b)	Tughlaq Dynasty	— Ghiyasuddin
(c)	Khilji Dynasty	— Jalaluddin
(d)	Lodi Dynasty	— Bahlul Lodi

28. Match the following.

	Dynasty		Founder
A.	Mughal Empire	1.	Ghiyasuddin Tughlaq
B.	Suri Dynasty	2.	Bahlol Lodhi
C.	Lodhi Dynasty	3.	Sher Shah
D.	Tughlaq Dynasty	4.	Babur

Codes

	A	B	C	D
(a)	1	2	3	4
(b)	2	3	1	4
(c)	4	1	2	3
(d)	4	3	2	1

Historical Monuments, Art and Architecture

1 Mark Questions

1. The Ajanta caves are located in ....
   (a) Karnataka   (b) Maharashtra
   (c) Uttar Pradesh (d) Andhra Pradesh

2. The Rock edicts were erected in his kingdom by which king?
   (a) Akbar
   (b) Chandragupta Maurya
   (c) Ashoka
   (d) Balban

3. Which among the following is the example of Nagara Style architecture?
   (a) Rajarani Temple (b) Red Fort
   (c) Taj Mahal   (d) Qutub Minar

4. Warli painting is indigenous to which states?
   (a) Gujarat   (b) Rajasthan
   (c) Odisha   (d) Maharashtra

5. Which of the following monuments is located in Thanjavur, Tamil Nadu?
   (a) Brihadisvara Temple
   (b) Sanchi Stupa
   (c) Hampi
   (d) Red Fort

6. The city famous for its Chikankari work of embroidery is ....
   (a) Lucknow   (b) Delhi
   (c) Kolkata   (b) Kanpur

7. The monuments of Khajuraho was built by ....
   (a) Chandela dynasty
   (b) Parmar dynasty
   (c) Tomar dynasty
   (d) Chauhan dynasty

8. Madhubani paintings is famous painting form of ....
   (a) Bihar   (b) Uttar Pradesh
   (c) Jharkhand (d) Odisha

9. Which heritage site depicts the fine Dravidian art and architecture?
   (a) Akshardham (b) Khajuraho
   (c) Hampi   (d) Ajanta

10. Which caves are well known for their Indian-rock cut architecture?
    (a) Ajanta   (b) Ellora
    (c) Hampi   (d) Khajuraho

11. Charminar, located in Hyderabad was built by ....
    (a) Adil Shah
    (b) Qutub Shah
    (c) Shah Jahan
    (d) Muhammad bin Tughlaq

12. Which of the following monuments is Indo-Islamic monument?
    (a) Jama Masjid
    (b) Golden Temple
    (c) Hampi
    (d) Ellora

13. The famous Jaina monument, Dilwara Temple is located in which of the following states?
    (a) Gujarat
    (b) Rajasthan
    (c) Madhya Pradesh
    (d) Maharashtra

14. Which among the following monuments is located in Odisha?
    (a) Konark Sun Temple
    (b) Lotus Temple
    (c) Hawa Mahal
    (d) Golkonda Fort

15. Jantar Mantar is located in which of the following states?
    (a) Rajasthan
    (b) Gujarat
    (c) Madhya Pradesh
    (d) Karnataka

16. .... is a classical dance form of Uttar Pradesh.
    (a) Kathak
    (b) Kuchipudi
    (c) Kathakali
    (d) Gidda

17. The indigenous dance form of Assam is ....
    (a) Dasavattar
    (b) Bihu
    (c) Kalbelia
    (d) Gidda

18. Hawa Mahal was built by ....
    (a) Maharaja Sawai Pratap Singh
    (b) Rana Kumbha
    (c) Maharana Pratap Singh
    (c) Maharaja Surajmal

19. The Taj Mahal is located in ....
    (a) Agra
    (b) Lucknow
    (c) Delhi
    (d) Mathura

20. Sanchi Stupa was built by which of the following rulers?
    (a) Ashoka
    (b) Bindusara
    (c) Skandagupta
    (d) Chandragupta Maurya

21. .... is performed in honour of Hindu goddesses and gods during Navratri.
    (a) Jhumar
    (b) Garba
    (c) Domkach
    (d) Bhangra

22. Which of the following is famous for the monumental architecture of Pallavas in Tamil Nadu?
    (a) Mahabalipuram
    (b) Nilgiri
    (c) Bada Imambada
    (d) Konark Sun Temple

23. The art of painting reached its climax during which Mughal Emperor's reign?
    (a) Akbar
    (b) Shah Jahan
    (c) Jahangir
    (d) Aurangzeb

2 Marks Questions

24. Which of the following statements is/are true?

1. Nalanda University is a UNESCO World Heritage site, located in Bihar.
2. It is considered as the oldest university of the world.

Codes
(a) Only 1
(b) Only 2
(c) Both 1 and 2
(d) None of the above

25. Which of the following is/are true?

1. Sun temple is considered one of the best examples of Dravidian architecture.
2. The Taj Mahal was built by Mughal emperor Shah Jahan in 1648.

Codes
(a) Only 1
(b) Only 2
(c) Both 1 and 2
(d) None of the above

26. Consider the following statements.

1. Warli paintings are famous art form of Maharashtra.
2. Chikankari is a popular art form of Lucknow.

Select the correct option from the codes given below.

Codes
(a) Only 1   (b) Only 2
(c) Both 1 and 2   (d) None of these

27. State T for true and F for false of the given statements.

A. Hawa Mahal was built by King Sawai Pratap Singh in 1799.
B. Golgumbaz is located in Bijapur, Karnataka.
C. Sanchi Stupa was built by Ashoka in Madhya Pradesh.

Codes

	A	B	C			A	B	C
(a)	F	F	F		(b)	T	T	T
(c)	T	T	T		(d)	F	F	T

28. Match the following.

Paintings/Art		State	
A.	Madhubani Painting	1.	Rajasthan
B.	Kalamkari Art	2.	Andhra Pradesh
C.	Miniature Painting	3.	Bihar

Codes

	A	B	C			A	B	C
(a)	1	2	3		(b)	3	2	1
(c)	1	3	2		(d)	3	1	2

Solar System

1 Mark Questions

1. The study of universe is known as ....
   (a) Cosmology   (b) Astrobiology
   (c) Aerology   (d) Astronomy

2. Which of the following planets in the Solar System takes the shortest revolution?
   (a) Neptune   (b) Mars
   (c) Mercury   (d) Venus

3. What are celestial bodies?
   (a) The Sun
   (b) The Moon
   (c) All the shining bodies in the sky
   (d) All of the above

4. The celestial bodies which have their own heat and light are called ....
   (a) Planets   (b) Stars
   (c) Satellites   (d) All of these

5. Which among the following is the most recognisable constellation?
   (a) The Moon
   (b) The Sun
   (c) The Mars
   (d) The Saptarishi

6. The Milky Way Galaxy is known as ....
   (a) Akash Ganga   (b) Nakshatra Ganga
   (c) Antariksha   (d) Vyom

7. The small pieces of rocks which move around the Sun are called ....
   (a) Meteoroids
   (b) Milky Way Galaxy
   (c) Asteroids
   (d) Satellite

8. Which planet in the Solar System has the highest density?
   (a) Earth   (b) Uranus
   (c) Neptune   (d) Jupiter

9. The Moon moves around the Earth in about .... days.
   (a) 25   (b) 27
   (c) 29   (d) 31

10. Which planet takes the highest time to revolve around the Sun?
    (a) Jupiter   (b) Neptune
    (c) Uranus   (d) Saturn

11. Which of the following is regarded as Dwarf planet?
    (a) Neptune   (b) Mars
    (c) Pluto   (d) Venus

12. Which of the following planet rotates at the fastest rate among the given planets?
    (a) Earth   (b) Jupiter
    (c) Mars   (d) Mercury

13. Which planet is known as 'Green planet'?
    (a) Uranus   (b) Jupiter
    (c) Neptune   (d) Pluto

14. Which small objects revolve around the orbits of Mars and Jupiter?
    (a) Satellites   (b) Comets
    (c) Asteroids   (d) Meteorites

15. Which planet has a runway greenhouse effect ?
    (a) Mars   (b) Neptune
    (c) Mercury   (d) Venus

16. Titan is the largest satellite of ....
    (a) Uranus   (b) Saturn
    (c) Jupiter   (d) Mercury

17. Which of the following part of the Sun is visible to humans?
    (a) Photosphere   (b) Corona
    (c) Chromosphere   (d) Core

18. Which planet has more moons than any other planet in the Solar System?
    (a) Jupiter   (b) Uranus
    (c) Neptune   (d) Saturn

19. .... is the only natural satellite of the Earth.
    (a) The Sun   (b) The Moon
    (c) Mercury   (d) Uranus

20. Which is the 'coldest planet'?
    (a) Jupiter   (b) Uranus
    (c) Venus   (d) Neptune

21. Which planet of Solar System is also known as 'Earth's twin'?
    (a) Mercury   (b) Mars
    (c) Venus   (d) Jupiter

22. Which of the following planet is nearest to the Earth?
    (a) Mercury   (b) Venus
    (c) Mars   (d) Jupiter

23. Which planet is the slowest to orbit the Sun?
    (a) Neptune   (b) Mercury
    (c) Venus   (d) Uranus

24. Proxima Centuari is the closest star of ....
    (a) the Earth   (b) the Moon
    (c) Solar System   (d) Venus

25. ...... occurs when the Moon comes between the Earth and the Sun.
    (a) Solar eclipse   (b) Lunar eclipse
    (c) Both (a) and (b)   (d) None of these

26. Lunar eclipse occurs during the ....
    (a) full moon phase
    (b) new moon phase
    (c) half moon phase
    (d) None of the above

2 Marks Questions

27. Which of the given statements is/are true?

1. The hottest planet of the Solar System is Mercury.
2. Mercury is made up of dense rock materials.

Codes
(a) Only 1   (b) Only 2
(c) Both 1 and 2   (d) None of these

28. Which of the following is true?

1. A Galaxy is a huge system that contains billions of stars, gases and clouds of dust.
2. The path in which planet or satellites moves around is called orbit.

Codes
(a) Only 1   (b) Only 2
(c) Both 1 and 2   (d) None of these

29. Which of the following is true?

1. A satellite is an object that moves around a planet.
2. Jupiter has the largest number of satellites.
3. Mars has only two natural satellites.

Codes
(a) Only 1 and 3
(b) Only 1 and 2
(c) Only 2 and 3
(d) 1, 2 and 3

30. State T for true and F for false for the given statements.

A. Comets revolve around the Earth in Solar System.
2. Stars produce their own light and heat.
3. The Asteroids revolve around the Sun in Solar System.

Codes

	A	B	C			A	B	C
(a)	T	F	T		(b)	F	T	F
(c)	F	T	T		(d)	T	T	T

31. Which is not correctly matched?
(a) Biggest planet-Jupiter
(b) Farthest planet from the Sun-Neptune
(c) Fastest rotation in Solar System-Jupiter
(d) Hottest planet-Mars

32. Match the List I with List II.

	List I		List II
A.	Green Planet	1.	Mercury
B.	Coldest Planet	2.	Neptune
C.	Morning Star	3.	Venus
D.	Smallest Planet	4.	Uranus

Codes

	A	B	C	D			A	B	C	D
(a)	4	2	3	1		(b)	1	2	3	4
(c)	4	3	2	1		(d)	3	1	4	2

Chapter 05

Our Earth

1 Mark Questions

1. The Globe and the Earth are different in ....
   (a) shape (b) size (c) tilt (d) poles

2. The Earth moves around its ....
   (a) Axis (b) Poles
   (c) Equator (d) Meridian

3. Which of the following imaginary line divides the Earth into two equal halves?
   (a) Equator (b) Pole
   (c) Longitude (d) Prime Meridian

4. The Arctic circle is located in the .... hemisphere.
   (a) Southern (b) Northern
   (c) Both (a) and (b) (d) None of these

5. Which of the following latitude is considered as the Tropic of Cancer?
   (a) $23\frac{1}{2}°$N (b) $66\frac{1}{2}°$N
   (c) $66\frac{1}{2}°$S (d) $23\frac{1}{2}°$S

6. The part of the Earth, where life exists is called ....
   (a) Biosphere (b) Hydrosphere
   (c) Lithosphere (d) Atmosphere

7. The time of India is ahead of Prime meridian by how many hours?
   (a) 6 hours 20 minutes
   (b) 3 hours 10 minutes
   (c) 7 hours 10 minutes
   (d) 5 hours 30 minutes

8. All parallel circles from the equator upto pole are called ....
   (a) Longitudes (b) Equator
   (c) Latitudes (d) Arctic circle

9. The area that receives maximum heat on Earth's surface is called ....
   (a) Torrid zone (b) Temperature zone
   (c) Frigid zone (d) All of these

10. In what direction the Earth spins on its axis?
    (a) West to East (b) West to West
    (c) North to South (d) South to North

11. The year with how many days is called leap year?
    (a) 365 (b) 366 (c) 367 (d) 364

12. The uppermost layer of the Earth's surface is called ....
    (a) the Crust
    (b) the Mantle
    (c) the Core
    (d) All of the above

13. The circle that divides the globe into day and night is called ....
(a) circle of day
(b) circle of night
(c) circle of illumination
(d) circle of darkness

14. The solid part of the Earth on which we live is called ....
(a) Lithosphere   (b) Atmosphere
(c) Biosphere   (d) Hydrosphere

15. The lowermost layer of Earth's atmosphere is known as ....
(a) Mesosphere   (b) Troposphere
(c) Hydrosphere   (d) Ozonosphere

16. .... shows natural feature of the Earth.
(a) Political map   (b) Physical map
(c) Thematic map   (d) None of these

17. Scale is a compulsory for ....
(a) globe   (b) a map
(c) a sketch   (d) a symbol

18. The movement of the Earth on its axis around the Sun is called ....
(a) Revolution   (b) Rotation
(c) Circle   (d) Orbital plane

19. What divides the Earth into Eastern and Western part?
(a) Prime Meridian
(b) Tropic of Capricorn
(c) Tropic of Cancer
(d) Axis of the Earth

20. The natural temperature of a place on Earth can be determined by its ....
(a) Longitude   (b) Latitude
(c) Rainfall   (d) Meridian

21. When do the longest day and shortest night occur in the Northern hemisphere?
(a) 21st June   (b) 23rd September
(c) 23rd December   (d) 21st March

22. The position of the Earth when it is nearest point to the Sun is called ....
(a) Aphelion   (b) Equinox
(c) Solstice   (d) Perihelion

2 Marks Questions

23. Which of the following is true ?
1. The Earth moves around its axis, which is an imaginary line.
2. The regions of moderate temperature on Earth's surface are called temperate zone.

Codes
(a) Only 1   (b) Only 2
(c) Both 1 and 2   (d) None of these

24. Which of the following is not true?
1. The uppermost layer of the Earth's crust is lithosphere.
2. Latitude and longitude are required to locate a place on the Earth.

Codes
(a) Only 1   (b) Only 2
(c) Both 1 and 2   (d) None of these

25. State T for true and F for false for the given statements.
A. The Earth moves in direction from West to East.
B. There are 24 time zones on the Earth.
C. An hour covers 15° of Longitude.

Codes

	A	B	C		A	B	C
(a)	F	T	T	(b)	T	T	T
(c)	F	F	F	(d)	T	F	T

Chapter 06

Continents and Oceans

1 Mark Questions

1. The deepest point of the world is located in which continent?
   (a) Africa   (b) Europe
   (c) North America   (d) Asia

2. Which continent is also called as Dark Continent?
   (a) North America   (b) Africa
   (c) Asia   (d) Europe

3. Which continent has the largest number of countries?
   (a) Europe   (b) Asia
   (c) Africa   (d) South America

4. The deepest point on the Earth is Mariana Trench in the ...... ocean.
   (a) Pacific   (b) Indian
   (c) Atlantic   (d) Arctic

5. The highest mountain peak on the Earth is ....
   (a) Godwin Austin   (b) Nanga Parbat
   (c) Mount Everest   (d) Kanchenjunga

6. Tropic of Cancer passes through which continent?
   (a) Asia   (b) Europe
   (c) North America   (d) Australia

7. The only planet through which Tropic of Cancer, Topic of Capricorn and Equator passes is ....
   (a) Australia   (b) Africa
   (c) Asia   (d) South America

8. The Arctic circle passes through .... continent.
   (a) Europe   (b) Africa
   (c) South America   (d) Australia

9. Which is the second largest continent after Asia?
   (a) Africa   (b) Australia
   (c) North America   (d) Europe

10. Name the only continent of the Earth with no countries present in it?
    (a) Oceania   (b) Artic
    (c) Antarctica   (d) None of these

11. The Sahara Desert, the world's largest hot desert is located in ....
    (a) Africa   (b) Australia
    (c) North America (d) Antarctica

12. ...... is the world's longest river flows through Africa.
    (a) Nile river   (b) Amazon river
    (c) Yangtze   (d) Mississippi

13. The continent of North America is linked to South America by ....
    (a) a straight   (b) an isthmus
    (c) a canal   (d) All of these

14. South America lies mostly in which hemisphere?
    (a) Northern   (b) Southern
    (c) Western   (d) Eastern

15. The Andes mountain located in which of the following continents?
    (a) South America   (b) North America
    (c) Europe   (d) Australia

16. Which of the following continent is the flattest continent on Earth?
    (a) Africa   (b) Australia
    (c) North America   (d) Asia

17. Which continent is called as Island continent?
    (a) Australia   (b) Europe
    (c) Antarctica   (d) North America

18. The South pole lies almost at the centre of which continent?
    (a) Australia   (b) South America
    (c) Antarctica   (d) Asia

19. Where is 97 per cent of the Earth's water found?
    (a) In oceans   (b) In lakes
    (c) Underground   (d) In seas

20. How many oceans are there in the world?
    (a) 5   (b) 6   (c) 7   (d) 8

21. North America and South America are separated by which of the following?
    (a) Suez Canal   (b) Panama Canal
    (c) Kra Canal   (d) None of these

22. The .... is the largest ocean of the world.
    (a) Pacific ocean
    (b) Atlantic ocean
    (c) Indian ocean
    (d) Arctic ocean

2 Marks Questions

23. Which of the following is correctly matched?
    1. Asia-Largest continent
    2. Africa-Second largest continent
    3. Australia-Smallest continent
    Codes
    (a) Only 1   (b) Both 1 and 2
    (c) 1, 2 and 3   (d) Only 3

24. Which of the following pairs is not correctly matched?
    (a) Largest ocean-Pacific ocean
    (b) Second largest ocean-Atlantic ocean
    (c) Circular shaped ocean-Indian ocean
    (d) Located within Arctic circle-Arctic ocean

25. Consider the following statements.
    1. Asia is separated from Europe by the ural mountains.
    2. North America is linked with South America by Carribean sea.
    3. The Andes mountain range is located in North America.
    Codes
    (a) Only 1 and 3   (b) Only 2
    (c) Only 2 and 3   (d) All of these

26. State T for true and F for false for the given statements.
    A. The continent South America is the smallest continent.
    B. South America has world's largest river, the Amazon.
    C. Continent of Australia is surrounded on all sides by the oceans and seas.
    Codes

	A	B	C			A	B	C
(a)	F	T	T		(b)	F	T	F
(c)	T	T	T		(d)	F	F	T

Our Country-Location and Physical Division

1 Mark Questions

1. India is situated in which hemisphere?
(a) Northern   (b) Southern
(c) Western   (d) Eastern

2. India is bounded by ....in the East.
(a) Arabian Sea
(b) Bay of Bengal
(c) Indian Ocean
(d) Himalaya

3. Which latitude divides India into two halves?
(a) 23°30′N   (b) 26°30′N
(c) 30 30′S   (d) 30° 30″S

4. There are .... countries that share land boundaries with India.
(a) eight   (b) seven
(c) ten   (d) None of these

5. Sri Lanka is separated from India by ....
(a) Malacca strait   (b) Palk strait
(c) Sunda strait   (d) Berring strait

6. What is the North-South extention from Kashmir to Kanyakumari?
(a) About 5600 km
(b) About 2900 km
(c) About 3200 km
(d) About 1600 km

7. Which of the following is the Northern mountain range of India?
(a) Himadri   (b) Satpura
(c) Nilgiri   (d) Vindhya

8. Which river does not flow in the Northern plains of India?
(a) Yamuna   (b) Kosi
(c) Ganga   (d) Krishna

9. The Sun rises about how many hours earlier in the East as compared to the West?
(a) 3 hours   (b) 2 hours
(c) 4 hours   (d) 5 hours

10. What is the approximate latitudinal extent of India from North to South?
(a) 15°   (b) 20°   (c) 30°   (d) 60°

11. Which of the following divisions lies to the South of great plains of India?
(a) Himalayas
(b) North East Hills
(c) Peninsula
(d) Lakshadweep Islands

12. The Sun rises two hours earlier in ....
(a) Arunachal Pradesh
(b) Gujarat
(c) Assam
(d) Manipur

13. At which place Alaknanda and Bhagirathi meet to form river Ganga?
    (a) Devprayag
    (b) Allahabad
    (c) Haridwar
    (d) Rishikesh

14. Which among the following is the longest river in India?
    (a) Ganga   (b) Yamuna
    (c) Godavari   (d) Narmada

15. Lakshadweep Islands are located in the......... .
    (a) Arabian sea
    (b) Indian ocean
    (c) Pacific ocean
    (d) Arctic ocean

16. Which river in India crosses the Tropic of Cancer twice?
    (a) Tapi river   (b) Jhelum river
    (c) Krishna river   (d) Mahi river

17. Which of the following river does not flows into Bay of Bengal?
    (a) Narmada   (b) Ganga
    (c) Krishna   (d) Godavari

18. Indira Col is the .... point of India.
    (a) Northernmost   (b) Southernmost
    (c) Easternmost   (d) Westernmost

19. Which border line separates India from China ?
    (a) McMahon Line
    (b) Radcliffe Line
    (c) Durand Line
    (d) None of the boave

20. The border line between India and Pakistan is ....
    (a) Blue Line   (b) Radcliffe Line
    (c) McMahon Line   (d) Durand Line

21. The Easternmost point of India is ....
    (a) Indira Col   (b) Kibithu
    (c) Ghuar Moti   (d) Indira Point

22. Which of the following rivers is the home for freshwater dolphins?
    (a) Brahamputra
    (b) Yamuna
    (c) Ganga
    (d) Kaveri

23. The largest river of South India is ....
    (a) Godavari   (b) Krishna
    (c) Cauvery   (d) Mahanadi

24. Which of the following rivers is not a tributary of the Ganga?
    (a) Gomati   (b) Gandak
    (c) Kosi   (d) Chambal

25. The Sunderban delta is formed where the rivers Ganga and ...... flow into the Bay of Bengal.
    (a) Yamuna   (b) Brahmaputra
    (c) Godavari   (d) Gandak

26. Which of the Indian peninsular river has the largest basin?
    (a) Ganga
    (b) Narmada
    (c) Godavari
    (d) Krishna

27. Which river is popularly known as Dakshin Ganga?
    (a) Krishna   (b) Godavari
    (c) Mahanadi   (d) Cauvery

28. Which is the Westernmost point of India?
    (a) Indira Col   (b) Indira Point
    (c) Ghuar Moti   (d) None of these

2 Marks Questions

29. State T for true and F for false for the given statements.

    A. The East-West extent of India is double of the North South extent.

    B. The local time changes by four minutes for every one degree of Longitude.

    Codes

	A	B			A	B
(a)	T	T	(b)		F	F
(c)	F	T	(d)		T	F

30. Which of the following statement is correct?

    1. The Thar desert is the largest hot desert of India.

    2. Thar desert is located on the West of Aravalli mountain range.

    Codes
    (a) Only 1   (b) Only 2
    (c) Both 1 and 2   (d) None of these

31. Which of the following statement is true?

    A. The Andaman and Nicobar islands are volcanic islands located in Arabian sea.

    B. Lakshadweep island group does not contain any volcano.

    Codes
    (a) Only 1   (b) Only 2
    (c) Both 1 and 2   (d) None of these

32. Which of the following is true?

    1. Sri Lanka and Maldives are island neighbours of India.

    2. The Palk Strait separates Sri Lanka from India.

    3. India shares its land boundary with four countries.

    Codes
    (a) Only 1   (b) Only 3
    (c) Both 1 and 2   (d) All of these

33. Consider the following statements.

    1. The Brahmaputra river originates in Tibet.

    2. The Godavari is the longest peninsular river of India.

    3. The rivers Jhelum and Chenab are the tributary of Indus river.

    Codes
    (a) Both 1 and 2   (b) Only 3
    (c) Both 1 and 3   (d) All of these

34. Match the following.

A.	Dakshin Ganga	1.	Godavari
B.	Longest river of India	2.	Ganga
C.	Tributary of Ganga	3.	Yamuna

    Codes

	A	B	C			A	B	C
(a)	1	2	3	(b)		3	2	1
(c)	2	3	1	(d)		3	1	2

Mountains, Plateaus and Plains

1 Mark Questions

1. The southernmost Himalayas are known as ....
(a) Shivalik (b) Himadri
(c) Himachal (d) Aravalli

2. The Himalayan mountains are divided into .... main parallel ranges.
(a) four (b) three
(c) six (d) five

3. The oldest mountain range in India is the ....
(a) Himalayas
(b) Western Ghats
(c) Aravalli Mountains
(d) Shivalik

4. The Greater Himalayas are also known as ....
(a) Himadri (b) Shivalik
(c) Western Ghats (d) Aravalli

5. Which of the following is the highest point of India?
(a) Mt. Everest (b) Kanchenjunga
(c) Karakoram (d) Shivalik

6. Pir Pranjal range in the Himalaya is a part of ....
(a) Shivalik (b) Trans Himalaya
(c) Lesser Himalaya (d) Middle Himalaya

7. The highest peak in the Eastern Ghats is ....
(a) Anai Mudi (b) Doda Betta
(c) Shivalik (d) Jhindhagada

8. Mount Everest, the highest peak in the world is located in which range?
(a) Himachal (b) Vindhya
(c) Shivalik (d) Himadri

9. The drainage system of Narmada and Son lies in the ....
(a) Aravalli Mountain
(b) Satpura Mountain
(c) Western Ghats
(d) Eastern Ghats

10. The river which divides the Peninsular plateau from Great Plains is ....
(a) Ganga (b) Narmada
(c) Godawari (d) Krishna

11. Dhupgarh is the highest point of ....
(a) Vindhya range   (b) Satpura range
(c) Aravalli   (d) Shivalik

12. Which of the following also known as Sahyadris?
(a) Western Ghats   (b) Eastern Ghats
(c) Himachal   (d) Himalaya

13. Himalayan mountains are example of ....
(a) Fold mountain
(b) Block mountain
(c) Volcanic mountain
(d) None of the above

14. The only volcanic mountain peak in India is located in ....
(a) Lakshadweep
(b) Andaman and Nicobar Island
(c) Karnataka
(d) Mizoram

15. Aravalli is an example of ....
(a) Young fold mountain
(b) Block mountain
(c) Old fold mountain
(d) Volcanic mountain

16. The Eastern Ghats and the Western Ghats meets at the ....
(a) Nilgiri hills   (b) Cardamom hills
(c) Annamalai hills (d) Nallamalla hills

17. The highest peak of Western Ghats is ....
(a) Meesapulimala (b) Doddabetta
(c) Anamudi   (d) Mahendragiri

18. Which is the southernmost mountain in India ?
(a) Cardamom hills (b) Nilgiri hills
(c) Annamalai hills (d) Sesachalam hills

19. The shape of Deccan Plateau in India is ....
(a) circular   (b) rectangular
(c) triangular   (d) None of these

20. Which of the following geographical regions can be considered as 'storehouse of mineral resource' in India?
(a) Gangetic plains
(b) Himalayan mountains
(c) Deccan plateau
(d) Indian desert

21. Which of the following deserts is located in India?
(a) Thar Desert   (b) Gobi Desert
(c) Sahara Desert   (d) Simpson Desert

22. Huge reserves of coal in India is found in ....
(a) Chhota Nagpur Plateau
(b) Malwa Plateau
(c) Karnataka Plateau
(d) None of the above

23. Which of the following geographical region constitutes largest area in India ?
(a) Plateau   (b) Mountain
(c) Desert   (d) Plain

24. Jog falls is located in ....
(a) Jharkhand
(b) Tamil Nadu
(c) Karnataka
(d) Madhya Pradesh

25. Which of the following mountain range of India is located in the plateau region?
(a) Himadri   (b) Shivaliks
(c) Karakoram   (d) Nilgiris

26. The mountains differ from plateau in ....
(a) base   (b) extension
(c) texture   (d) elevation

27. Famous tourist spots are mostly located in ....
(a) plains   (b) mountains
(c) plateaus   (d) valleys

28. Some of the largest plains made by the rivers are found in ....
    (a) Asia   (b) Europe
    (c) North America   (d) Australia

29. Which is the most useful area for human habitation?
    (a) Mountains   (b) Plateau
    (c) Plains   (d) All of these

2 Marks Questions

30. Which of the following is true?
    1. The highest mountain peak of World is in India.
    2. The longest river of the World is in India.

    Codes
    (a) Only 1   (b) Both 1 and 2
    (c) Only 2   (d) None of these

31. Consider the following statements about Himalayas?
    1. It is the longest mountain range in the world.
    2. It is the source of many perennial river.
    3. It lies in India and Nepal only.

    Codes
    (a) Only 1 and 2   (b) Only 1 and 3
    (c) Only 2   (d) All of these

32. State T for true and F for false for the given statements.
    A. The greater Himalayas are also known as Shivaliks.
    B. Hill is a land surface higher than surrounding area.
    C. The features of young fold mountains are rugged relief and high conical peak.

    Codes

	A	B	C			A	B	C
(a)	T	F	T		(b)	F	T	F
(c)	T	T	F		(d)	F	T	T

33. Which of the following statement is true?
    1. The Deccan plateau was formed from the cooling and solidification of Lava.
    2. The Satpura and Vindhya range forms the Northern boundary of Deccan plateau.

    Codes
    (a) Only 1   (b) Only 2
    (c) Both 1 and 2   (d) None of these

34. Which of the following pairs (hill ranges-state) is not correctly matched?
    (a) Aravalli   – Rajasthan
    (b) Vindhya   – Madhya Pradesh
    (c) Chhota Nagpur   – Gujarat
    (d) Western Ghats   – Karnataka

35. Match the following.

Physiographical Features		States	
A.	Himalayan Mountains	1.	Meghalaya
B.	Garo Hills	2.	Himachal Pradesh
C.	Thar Desert	3.	Odisha
D.	Eastern Ghats	4.	Rajasthan

    Codes

	A	B	C	D
(a)	2	1	3	4
(b)	1	4	2	3
(c)	3	4	1	2
(d)	2	1	4	3

Chapter 09

Climate and Vegetation

1 Mark Questions

1. Day to day changes in the atmosphere are known as ....
   (a) weather   (b) vegetation
   (c) climate   (d) None of these

2. .... is the average weather in a given area over a long period of time.
   (a) Climate   (b) Vegetation
   (c) Temperature   (d) Climate changes

3. The duration of cold season in India is ....
   (a) March to May
   (b) December to February
   (c) November to January
   (d) September to June

4. During the winter season, the Sun rays .... over the surface.
   (a) falls directly   (b) falls obliquely
   (c) perpendicular   (d) parallel

5. In which season, the temperature is quite low in Northern India?
   (a) Season of retreating monsoon
   (b) Hot weather season
   (c) South-West monsoon season
   (d) Cold weather season

6. Andhra Pradesh and Tamil Nadu receive a great amount of rainfall during the season of ....
   (a) retreating monsoon (b) monsoon
   (c) summer   (d) winter

7. Hot and dry winds are called ....
   (a) hot air   (b) breeze
   (c) loo   (d) air

8. The highest amount of rainfall in world occurs in ....
   (a) Mumbai   (b) Nagaland
   (c) Mawsynram   (d) Asansol

9. The places which experience moderate climate are ....
   (a) Mumbai and Kolkata
   (b) Patna and Lucknow
   (c) Bikaner and Jaisalmer
   (d) Ranchi and Asansol

10. .... forest can survive in saline water.
    (a) Mangrove   (b) Deciduous
    (c) Tundra   (d) Evergreen

11. Mahogany and rosewood trees are found in ....
    (a) Tropical Evergreen Forests
    (b) Tropical Deciduous Forests
    (c) Mangrove Forests
    (d) Mountain Forests

12. Tropical Deciduous Forests are also called ....
    (a) Mountain forest
    (b) Hot forest
    (c) Desert forest
    (d) Monsoon forest

13. The Tropical Rain Forests are found in which of the following region of India?
    (a) Northern Himalaya
    (b) Thar Desert
    (c) Western Ghats
    (d) Gangetic Plains

14. Sundarbans is located in ....
    (a) Kerala
    (b) West Bengal
    (c) Assam
    (d) Arunachal Pradesh

15. Which of the following acts as the barrier to rains causing winds ?
    (a) Sea   (b) River
    (c) Mountain   (d) Plateau

16. During the night time which gas is released by the plants?
    (a) Oxygen   (b) Carbon Dioxide
    (c) Hydrogen   (d) Nitrogen

17. Mangrove forests are found in ....
    (a) West Bengal   (b) Madhya Pradesh
    (c) Kerala   (d) Rajasthan

2 Marks Questions

18. Which of the following is not true?
    1. December to February is cold weather season.
    2. Hot and dry winds called loo, blow during day in hot weather season.

    Codes
    (a) Only 1   (b) Only 2
    (c) Both 1 and 2   (d) Neither 1 nor 2

19. State T for true and F for false in the given statements.
    A. Mangrove forests can survive even in saline water.
    B. It is found mainly in Sundarbans West Bengal.
    C. Sundari species is found in Mangrove forests.

    Codes

	A	B	C			A	B	C
(a)	F	F	F		(b)	T	F	T
(c)	T	T	T		(d)	F	T	F

20. Which of the given statement is correct?
    1. India gets more than 50% of its rainfall in the monsoon season.
    2. Climate of South India is more hot as compared to North India.

    Codes
    (a) Only 1   (b) Only 2
    (c) Both 1 and 2   (d) All of these

21. Which of the following statement is true regarding Indian climate?
    1. The coastal areas of India have moderate climate.
    2. Northwestern region of India has dry climate.
    3. Northeastern region of India has rainy climate.

    Codes
    (a) Only 1 and 2
    (b) Only 2 and 3
    (c) Both 1 and 3
    (d) All of the above

22. Which of the following functions is performed by natural vegetation?
    1. Prevent soil erosion
    2. Providing timber and fodder
    3. Preventing Tsunami

    Codes
    (a) Only 1 and 2   (b) Only 1 and 3
    (c) Both 2 and 3   (d) All of these

Ecology and Environment

1 Mark Questions

1. The natural residence of every organism is called ....
   (a) Biome   (b) Niche
   (c) Habitat   (d) Habit

2. Wide variety of living organism is called ....
   (a) Biodiversity   (b) Ecosystem
   (c) Habitat   (d) Diversity

3. Which of the following requires maximum energy?
   (a) Second consumer
   (b) Decomposer
   (c) Primary consumer
   (d) Primary producer

4. Grass that gains energy from the Sun is an example of ....
   (a) Consumer   (b) Parasite
   (c) Decomposer   (d) Producer

5. .... is the primary source of energy in all ecosystems.
   (a) Plants   (b) The Sun
   (c) Producers
   (d) Animals

6. Environment includes ....
   (a) abiotic component
   (b) biotic component
   (c) Both (a) and (b)
   (d) None of the above

7. The largest ecosystem of Earth is ....
   (a) Biome   (b) Hydrosphere
   (c) Lithosphere   (d) Biosphere

8. The main cause for melting of ice-sheets is ....
   (a) Global warming
   (b) Pollution
   (c) Increase in the oxygen
   (d) All of the above

9. The term ecosystem was proposed by ....
   (a) Lindeman   (b) Tansley
   (c) Grinnell   (d) Turesson

10. Bandipur Tiger Reserve and National Park is located in ....
    (a) Bihar   (b) Karnataka
    (c) Kerala   (d) Tamil Nadu

11. Similipal National Park is located in which state?
    (a) Odisha (b) Rajasthan
    (c) Gujarat (d) Jharkhand

12. Elephants and one-horned rhinoceroses are found in the forests of ....
    (a) Assam (b) Gujarat
    (c) Kerala (d) Karnataka

13. The Nanda Devi National Park is located in ....
    (a) Uttarakhand
    (b) Himachal Pradesh
    (c) Jammu and Kashmir
    (d) Karnataka

14. Acid rain is a result of ....
    (a) excess amount of CO_2
    (b) excess amount of NH_3
    (c) excess amount of SO_2 and NO_2
    (d) excess amount of CO

15. Which of the following initiative was launched by Government to protect tiger population in 1973?
    (a) Preserve Tiger (b) Save Tiger
    (c) Project Tiger (d) Tiger Safe

16. Which Wildlife Bird Sanctuary is located in Rajasthan?
    (a) Bharatpur Bird Sanctuary
    (b) Chilka Bird Sanctuary
    (c) Udhwa Wildlife Sanctuary
    (d) Nawabganj Bird Sanctuary

17. The largest National Park of India is ....
    (a) Hemis National Park
    (b) Gangotri National Park
    (c) Gir Forest National Park
    (d) Kaziranga National Park

18. Gulf of Mannar Biosphere reserve is located in ....
    (a) Uttarakhand
    (b) Tamil Nadu
    (c) Odisha
    (d) West Bengal

19. Which biosphere reserve is located in Madhya Pradesh?
    (a) Panna Biosphere Reserve
    (b) Nilgiri Biosphere Reserve
    (c) Sundarbans Biosphere Reserve
    (d) Gulf of Mannar

20. Which national park has the largest population of Royal Bengal Tiger?
    (a) Sundarbans National Park
    (b) Jim Corbett National Park
    (c) Kanha National Park
    (d) All of the above

21. The endangered Asiatic lions found in which National Park?
    (a) Kaziranga National Park
    (b) Gir National Park
    (c) Ranthambore National Park
    (d) Jim Corbett National Park

22. Which of the following is not one of 3 'r's of recycling?
    (a) Recycle
    (b) Reverse
    (c) Reduce
    (d) Reuse

23. The first biosphere reserve of India is ....
    (a) Nilgiri
    (b) Nanda Devi
    (c) Manas
    (d) Gulf of Mannar

2 Marks Questions

24. Which of the following is not correctly matched?

(a) Jim Corbett National Park– Jharkhand
(b) Hemis National Park–Jammu and Kashmir
(c) Kaziranga National Park–Assam
(d) Valley of Flowers National Park– Uttarakhand

25. Which of the following is not true?

1. Environment means anything that surrounds us.
2. Biotic components are living factors of an ecosystem.

Codes
(a) Only 1
(b) Only 2
(c) Both 1 and 2
(d) Neither 1 nor 2

26. Consider the following statements.

1. Forests are home to a variety of wildlife.
2. Gir forest in Gujarat is the home of Asiatic lions.
3. Largest number of Tigers are located in Madhya Pradesh

Codes
(a) Only 1　　　　(b) Only 2
(c) Both 1 and 3　(d) All of these

27. Which of the following is/are true?

1. National Parks are the areas that are set by the Government to conserve the biodiversity.
2. Project Elephant was launched in 1992 by the Government of India.

Codes
(a) Only 1　　　　(b) Only 2
(c) Both 1 and 2　(d) None of these

28. State T for true and F for false for the given statements.

A. Abiotic components are non-living chemical and physical factors of an ecosystem.
B. Examples of biotic components include sunlight, soil, air, moisture, minerals and more.

Codes

	A	B			A	B
(a)	F	F		(b)	T	T
(c)	F	T		(d)	T	F

29. State T for true and F for false for the given statements.

1. The Kaziranga National Park is the largest National Park of India.
2. It is located in Jammu and Kashmir.
3. Jim Corbett National Park is the first National Park established in India.

Codes

	A	B	C			A	B	C
(a)	F	T	F		(b)	T	F	T
(c)	F	T	T		(d)	F	F	T

30. Match the following.

	List I		List II
A.	Dachigam Wildlife Sanctuary	1.	Jammu and Kashmir
B.	Manas Wildlife Sanctuary	2.	Assam
C.	Periyar Wildlife Sanctuary	3.	Kerala

Codes

	A	B	C			A	B	C
(a)	1	2	3		(b)	3	2	1
(c)	2	3	1		(d)	2	1	3

Indian Constitution

1 Mark Questions

1. Who was the Chairman of the Drafting Committee of Constituent Assembly?
   (a) Jawaharlal Nehru
   (b) B.R. Ambedkar
   (c) Mahatma Gandhi
   (d) Rajendra Prasad

2. The first Supreme Court was established at which place?
   (a) Delhi
   (b) Bombay
   (c) Chennai
   (d) Kolkata

3. Indian Constitution Assembly was established under………． .
   (a) Government of India Act
   (b) Cripps Mission
   (c) Cabinet Mission
   (d) Indian Independence Act

4. There are ……… Fundamental Rights in the Constitution of India.
   (a) 6   (b) 5
   (c) 8   (d) 11

5. The mind of the makers of the Constitution of India is reflected in which of the following?
   (a) The Preamble
   (b) The Fundamental Right
   (c) The DPSP
   (d) The Fundamental Duties

6. Who was the first Chairman of Constituent Assembly?
   (a) Dr. B.R. Ambedkar
   (b) Dr. Sachidanand Sinha
   (c) Dr. Rajendra Prasad
   (d) Dr. S Radhakrishnan

7. The Chairman of Steering Committee of Indian Constituent Assembly was ……. .
   (a) Dr. Rajendra Prasad
   (b) Jawaharlal Nehru
   (c) Dr. B.R. Ambedkar
   (d) Purushotam Das Tandan

8. How many parts are there in Indian Constitution?
   (a) 18   (b) 20   (c) 22   (d) 25

9. Which one of the following is the introduction or preface of the Constitution?
   (a) Secular State
   (b) Preamble
   (c) Judiciary
   (d) Fundamental Duties

10. Which Schedule of Indian Constitution distributes power between the Union and States?
    (a) First Schedule   (b) Second Schedule
    (c) Sixth Schedule   (d) Seventh Schedule

11. Right to Property is a ....
    (a) Moral Right
    (b) Fundamental Right
    (c) Legal Right
    (d) Personal Right

12. The concept of single citizenship in the Indian Constitution is inspired by which country?
    (a) Germany   (b) France
    (c) Ireland   (d) England

13. The Eighth Schedule of the Indian Constitution deals with ....
    (a) Anti-Defection Law
    (b) Languages
    (c) Allocation of the seat in Rajya Sabha
    (d) None of the above

14. The date of adoption of the Constitution is ....
    (a) 26th November, 1949
    (b) 26th January, 1950
    (c) 15th August, 1947
    (d) 30th January, 1960

15. Which of the 3 words were added later to the Preamble?
    (a) Justice, Liberty, Equality
    (b) Socialist, Republic, Justice
    (c) Sovereign, Fraternity, Political
    (d) Secular, Socialist, Integrity

16. The idea of 'Fundamental Duties' in the Indian Constitution is taken from the Constitution of ....
    (a) Russia   (b) Canada
    (c) Australia   (d) Japan

17. The Parliamentary form of government is borrowed From ....
    (a) Britain   (b) United States
    (c) Japan   (d) Australia

18. How many Fundamental Duties are there in Indian Constitution?
    (a) 11   (b) 6   (c) 9   (d) 10

19. Which country has the lengthiest Constitution in the world?
    (a) United States   (b) France
    (c) India   (d) Japan

20. The Fifth Schedule of the Constitution deals with ....
    (a) Schedule Areas
    (b) Fundamental Rights
    (c) Citizenship
    (d) Language

21. Which Article in the Constitution provides guidelines for amending the Preamble?
    (a) Article 30   (b) Article 200
    (c) Article 368   (d) Article 256

22. The Constitution of India is ....
    (a) rigid
    (b) flexible
    (c) combination of rigidity and flexibility
    (d) None of the above

23. Who among the following is known as Father of the Indian Constitution?
    (a) B.R. Ambedkar
    (b) Mahatma Gandhi
    (c) M.N. Roy
    (d) Jawaharlal Nehru

24. The idea of 'Directive Principles of State Policy' is borrowed from ....
    (a) Ireland   (b) United States
    (c) British   (d) Canada

25. The ideas of liberty, equality, and fraternity are taken from ....
(a) United States
(b) Spain
(c) Greece
(d) France

26. Which of the following is a fundamental duty?
(a) Protect natural environment
(b) Promote harmony among all
(c) Protect public property
(d) All of the above

2 Marks Questions

27. Which of the following statement is true?

1. There are currently 22 Parts in the Indian Constitution.

2. There are 12 Schedules in the Indian Constitution.

Codes
(a) Only 1
(b) Only 2
(c) Both 1 and 2
(d) None of these

28. Which of the following is matched incorrectly?

List I	List II
A. Fundamental Rights	— USA
B. DPSP	— Ireland
C. Fundamental Duties	— UK

Codes
(a) Only 1
(b) Only 2
(c) Only 3
(d) All of these

29. Which of the following is a fundamental duty of every citizen?
(a) To safeguard public property
(b) To uphold and protect the unity and integrity
(c) To respect National Flag and National Anthem
(d) All of the above

30. State T fore true and F for false for the given statements.

A. There are six Fundamental Duties in Indian Constitution.

B. The idea of Fundamental Duties is inspired from the Constitution of Russia.

Codes

	A	B			A	B
(a)	F	T		(b)	T	F
(c)	F	F		(d)	T	T

31. Consider the following statements and select the incorrect option.

1. The idea to have a Constitution was first given by MN Roy.

2. K.M. Munshi is known as the Father of Indian Constitution.

3. The idea of 'Rule of Law' was taken from United Kingdom.

Codes
(a) Only 1
(b) Both 2 and 3
(c) Both 1 and 3
(d) Only 2

32. Which of the following statement is correct?

1. Right to Education is a Fundamental Right given in the Constitution.

2. It is the Fundamental Duty of parents to provide education to their children.

Codes
(a) Only 1
(b) Only 2
(c) Both 1 and 2
(d) None of the above

Chapter 12

Our Government

1 Mark Questions

1. The Indian Parliament consists of ....
(a) Lok Sabha
(b) Rajya Sabha
(c) President
(d) All of the above

2. In a Parliamentary system, the Executive is responsible to ....
(a) Judiciary
(b) Legislature
(c) The People
(d) None of the above

3. Which of the following is the Lower House of Parliament?
(a) Rajya Sabha
(b) Lok Sabha
(c) Legislative Assembly
(d) Legislative Council

4. The Cabinet is responsible to .... in a Parliamentary form of Government.
(a) the nominal executive
(b) the Judiciary
(c) the Legislature
(d) None of the above

5. Minister is responsible for which among the following in a Parliamentary form of Government?
(a) Upper House
(b) Parliament
(c) Lower House
(d) Nominal Head of the state

6. .... is not associated with the Presidential Government.
(a) Administrative efficiency
(b) Stability
(c) Irresponsibility
(d) None of the above

7. Who among the following is not a member of any of the two houses of the Parliament?
(a) Prime Minister (b) President
(c) Railway Minister (d) Finance Minister

8. What is the minimum age requirement to become a member of the Legislative Assembly?
(a) 32 years (b) 25 years
(c) 20 years (d) 28 years

9. The Prime Minister is appointed by who among of the following?
   (a) Attorney General of India
   (b) President
   (c) Vice-President
   (d) Chief Justice of India

10. If the President has to resign, he gives his resignation to ....
    (a) Prime Minister   (b) Finance Minister
    (c) Vice-President   (d) Speaker

11. Who among the following heads the Central Government in India?
    (a) President
    (b) Prime Minister
    (c) Attorney General
    (d) Speaker of the Lok Sabha

12. Impeachment of the President can be initiated ....
    (a) only in Lok Sabha
    (b) only in Rajya Sabha
    (c) in either House of Parliament
    (d) in Supreme Court

13. Who investigates all the disputes related to the Vice-presidential election?
    (a) Parliament
    (b) Supreme Court
    (c) Election Commission
    (d) Both (b) and (c)

14. What is the minimum age for becoming member of the Lok Sabha?
    (a) 18 years   (b) 21 years
    (c) 25 years   (d) 30 years

15. How many sessions of the Lok Sabha generally takes place in a year?
    (a) 2   (b) 3   (c) 4   (d) 5

16. .... is known as the Father of Lok Sabha.
    (a) D. Balram Jakhar
    (b) GV Mavalankar
    (c) Rabi Ray
    (d) PA Sangma

17. What is the maximum strength (number of members) of the Lok Sabha mentioned by the Constitution?
    (a) 552   (b) 530
    (c) 555   (d) 545

18. Who administers the oath of affirmation of the Speaker of Lok Sabha?
    (a) President of India
    (b) Chief Justice of the Supreme Court
    (c) Senior most member of the Lok Sabha
    (d) None of the above

19. Who calls 'the Joint Session of the Parliament?
    (a) The President of India
    (b) Lok Sabha Speaker itself
    (c) Deputy Speaker of Lok Sabha
    (d) Prime Minister of India

20. Lok Sabha Speaker submits his resignation to ....
    (a) The President of India
    (b) The Deputy Speaker of the Lok Sabha
    (c) Chief Justice of India
    (d) Prime Minister of India

21. What is the minimum age to be appointed as the Chief Minister of a state?
    (a) 25 years
    (b) 30 years
    (c) 35 years
    (d) 18 years

22. The State Council of minister is responsible to whom?
    (a) To the Governor
    (b) To the Legislative Assembly
    (c) To the Legislative Council
    (d) To the State Legislature

23. Who provides oath to other ministers of the state other than the Chief Minister?
    (a) Chief Minister
    (b) Speaker of the assembly
    (c) Chief Justice of the High Court
    (d) Governor

2 Marks Questions

24. Which of the following statement is true?
    1. The President of India is elected directly by the people.
    2. The minimum age to contest Presidential election is 35 years.

    Codes
    (a) Only 1   (b) Only 2
    (c) Only 1 and 2   (d) None of these

25. Which of the following is true?
    1. Lok Sabha is the Lower House of the Parliament.
    2. Rajya Sabha is permanent body and not subject to dissolution.

    Codes
    (a) Only 1   (b) Only 2
    (c) Both 1 and 2   (d) None of these

26. Which of the following is/are true?
    1. Speaker of Lok Sabha is elected by Lok Sabha from amongst its members.
    2. A Governor is the Constitutional Head of the state.

    Codes
    (a) Only 1   (b) Only 2
    (c) Both 1 and 2   (d) Neither 1 nor 2

27. State T for true and F for false for the given statements.
    1. Chief Minister's tenure is not fixed.
    2. If the Chief Minister resigns from his post then the entire Council of Ministers has to resign.
    3. The collective responsibility of the Council of Ministers is to the State Legislature.

    Codes

	A	B	C			A	B	C
(a)	T	T	T		(b)	F	T	F
(c)	T	T	F		(d)	F	F	T

28. Which of the given statement is true?
    1. The Governor of a state is appointed by the Chief Minister.
    2. The Governor is the head of the government in the state.

    Codes
    (a) Only 1   (b) Only 2
    (c) Both 1 and 2   (d) None of these

29. Which is correctly matched?

1.	First Citizen of India	President
2.	Chairman of Rajya Sabha	Vice-President
3.	Prime Minister	Head of the Government

    Codes
    (a) Only 1   (b) Only 2
    (c) Both 1 and 3   (d) All of these

Chapter 13

Local Government and Administration

1 Mark Questions

1. The decision to conduct Panchayat elections is taken by which of the following?
   (a) Central Government
   (b) State Government
   (c) District Judge
   (d) Election Commission

2. The tenure of a Mayor is of ....
   (a) 1 years   (b) 2 years
   (c) 3 years   (d) 5 years

3. Who amongst the following is considered to be 'Father of Local Government' in India?
   (a) Lord Dalhousie   (b) Lord Canning
   (c) Lord Curzon   (d) Lord Ripon

4. Gram Panchayat members are elected by the ....
   (a) District Panchayat (b) Chief Minister
   (c) President   (d) Gram Sabha

5. The subject of Panchayati Raj falls under .... list of the Constitution.
   (a) State List   (b) Concurrent List
   (c) Union List   (d) All of these

6. The first state to implement the constitutional Panchayati Raj System is ....
   (a) Madhya Pradesh (b) Punjab
   (c) Andhra Pradesh (d) Rajasthan

7. The decision to conduct Panchayat elections is taken by which of the following?
   (a) The Central Government
   (b) The State Government
   (c) The District Judge
   (d) The State Election Commission

8. .... is a committee of five elderly, responsible persons of a village.
   (a) Zila Parishad
   (b) Panchayat Samiti
   (c) Panchayat
   (d) Gram Sabha

9. Who is a member of the Gram Sabha?
   (a) All teachers of village
   (b) All villagers
   (c) Every villager who has the right to vote
   (d) All the women members of village

10. Who is the President of Panchayat?
   (a) Panch
   (b) Ward members
   (c) Sarpanch
   (d) Member of Parliament

11. Which of the following is the top most tier of Panchayati Raj System?
   (a) Gram Panchayat (b) Panchayati Raj
   (c) Zila Parishad   (d) Panchayat Samiti

12. At which level does Zila Parishad actually makes development plans?
   (a) District level   (b) Village level
   (c) Block level   (d) Central level

13. Which of the following was constituted under the Panchayati Raj System?
   (a) Khap Panchayat (b) Caste Panchayat
   (c) Gram Panchayat (d) Jan Panchayat

14. Which of the following parts of the Constitution is related to the municipalities in urban areas?
   (a) Part VI   (b) Part VII
   (c) Part VIII   (d) Part IX-A

15. 'National Panchayati Raj Day' in India is observed on ....
   (a) 26th January   (b) 2nd October
   (c) 21st April   (d) 24th April

16. The Fundamental object of Panchayati Raj System is to ensure which among the following?
   (a) Peoples's participation in development
   (b) Inclusive development
   (c) Democratic decentralisation
   (d) All of the above

17. Who is considered as the Architect of Panchayati Raj in India?
   (a) BR Mehta   (b) LM Singhvi
   (c) GVK Rao   (d) Santhanam

18. Who is incharge of a police station in a village?
   (a) SP   (b) DIG   (c) DC   (d) SHO

19. Who measures land and keeps land records?
   (a) Tehsildar   (b) District Collector
   (c) Lekhpal   (d) Farmer

2 Marks Questions

20. Which of the following is true?
   1. The Gram Panchayat is elected for 5 years.
   2. Every Village Panchayat is divided into wards.
   Codes
   (a) Only 1   (b) Only 2
   (c) Both 1 and 2   (d) None of these

21. State T for true and F for false for the given statements.
   A. The main work of Patwari is measuring land and keeping records of land.
   B. Tehsildars are also known as the Revenue Officer.
   C. District Collector is the head of administration in a district.
   Codes

A	B	C		A	B	C
(a) T	F	T	(b) F	T	F
(c) T	T	T	(d) F	F	T

22. Which of the following is correctly matched?
   1. Gram Sabha — Sarpanch
   2. Block level — Panchayat Samiti
   3. District level — Zila Parishad
   Codes
   (a) Only 1   (b) Only 2
   (c) Both 1 and 3   (d) All of these

Science and Technology

1 Mark Questions

1. 'Light-year' is a unit of ....
   (a) Distance   (b) Time
   (c) Speed   (d) Force

2. Richard Jordan Gatling was the inventor of ....
   (a) Jet engine   (b) Lift
   (c) Machine Gun   (d) Motor Car

3. Laws of Motion were propounded by ..... .
   (a) Coulomb   (b) Newton
   (c) Einstein   (d) Mandelev

4. Who invented Transformer?
   (a) Faraday   (b) Einstein
   (c) Parsons   (d) CRT Wilson

5. Which of the following scientists is the inventor of the lift?
   (a) F.G. Otis
   (b) Edison
   (c) William Gas Cogin
   (d) Einstein

6. Who among the following scientists discovered the Gramophone?
   (a) Einstein   (b) Edison
   (c) John & John   (d) Janson & Janson

7. Radio is invented by Marconi, he was from ....
   (a) USA   (b) England
   (c) Germany   (d) France

8. The SI unit of power is ....
   (a) Watt   (b) Volt
   (c) Ohm   (d) Farad

9. The 'Second Law of Motion' gives the measure of which of the following?
   (a) Momentum   (b) Force
   (c) Acceleration   (d) Velocity

10. Which of the following is most reactive metal?
    (a) Sodium   (b) Calcium
    (c) Iron   (d) Potassium

11. The non-metal which is liquid at room temperature is ....
    (a) Mercury   (b) Bromine
    (c) Carbon   (d) Helium

12. Bauxite is an ore of ....
    (a) Iron   (b) Aluminium
    (c) Mercury   (d) Copper

13. .... is called White Gold.
(a) Platinum   (b) Copper
(c) Silver   (d) Bronze

14. Who among the following scientists is associated with discovery of electron?
(a) Galileo   (b) Einstein
(c) JJ Thomson   (d) DCRT Wilson

15. The chemical name of Bleaching powder is ....
(a) calcium hypochloride
(b) calcium oxychloride
(c) calcium chloride
(d) calcium chloro oxide

16. The acid used for the manufacturing of fertilizers and explosives is ....
(a) nitric acid
(b) sulfuric acid
(c) phosphoric acid
(d) hydrochloric acid

17. Fireworks release energy in the form of ....
(a) heat   (b) sound
(c) light   (d) All of these

18. Elements which have properties of metals and non-metals are ....
(a) amorphous   (b) crystalline
(c) metalloids   (d) metals

19. Loss of hydrogen atoms by an element is called ....
(a) hydrogenation   (b) oxidation
(c) reduction   (d) sublimation

20. Ultraviolet radiations from sunlight cause a reaction producing ....
(a) carbon monoxide
(b) ozone
(c) fluorides
(d) sulphur dioxide

21. Which nutrient provides the greatest energy value per gram of nutrient?
(a) Protein   (b) Fat
(c) Carbohydrate   (d) Water

22. Which of the following is a viral disease?
(a) Rickets   (b) Measles
(c) Beri-beri   (d) Syphilis

23. The source of carbon for plants in the carbon cycle is ....
(a) fossil fuels
(b) carbonate rocks
(c) atmospheric carbon dioxide
(d) All of the above

24. The study of internal structure of organism is known as ....
(a) Arthrology   (b) Anatomy
(c) Biotechnology   (d) Dermatology

25. Which of the following disease may be caused due to deficiency of vitamin A?
(a) Rickets
(b) Anaemia
(c) Colour Blindness
(d) Hairfall

26. Which mineral or vitamin should be taken in good amount to prevent osteomoalacia in adults?
(a) Vitamin K   (b) Vitamin A
(c) Vitamin D   (d) Sodium

27. Which among the following disease is caused by virus?
(a) Cholera   (b) Tuberculosis
(c) Polio   (d) Fungal infection

28. Which is the largest gland of Human body?
(a) Liver   (b) Gall Bladder
(c) Pancreas   (d) Lymph

2 Marks Questions

29. Consider the following statements.

1. Radar is a device used to determine the distant objects.

2. Radar uses a transmitter operating at either radio or microwave frequencies to emit electromagnetic radiation.

Choose the correct answer from the codes given below :

(a) Only 1   (b) Only 2

(c) Both 1 and 2   (d) Neither 1 nor 2

30. State T for true and F for false for the given statements.

1. The earlier televisions were made up of Cathode Ray Tubes (CRT).

2. The LED and LCD televisions are thinner than CRT televisions.

3. LED Technology uses more electricity than CRT.

Codes

	1	2	3			1	2	3
(a)	T	T	T		(b)	T	F	F
(c)	T	T	F		(d)	F	T	T

31. Which is not correctly matched?

(a) Bicycle – Macmillan

(b) Computer – Charles Babbage

(c) Scooter – James Watt

(d) Gramophone – T A Edison

32. Which of the given pair is matched correctly?

	Instrument	Measures
1.	Odometer	Distance
2.	Ammeter	Electric Current
3.	Barometer	Speed

Codes

(a) Only 2 and 3   (b) Only 1 and 2

(c) Only 1 and 3   (d) All of these

33. Which is correctly matched?

	Quantity	SI unit
1.	Pressure	Pascal
2.	Electric charge	Coulomb
3.	Force	Hertz

Codes

(a) Only 1   (b) Only 2

(c) Both 1 and 2   (d) All of these

34. Which of the given statement is true?

1. Sound can travel through vaccum.

2. Televisions and mobile phones can produce ultrasonic sounds.

3. The speed of light is more than speed of sound.

Codes

(a) Only 1 and 2   (b) Only 2

(c) Only 2 and 3   (d) Only 3

15

Computers

1 Mark Questions

1. Which of the following refers to a small, single site network?
   (a) LAN   (b) CPU
   (c) RAM   (d) USB

2. Computer equipment itself is called ....
   (a) Hardware   (b) Software
   (c) Default   (d) Processor

3. Which of the following is not an input device?
   (a) Keyboard   (b) Mouse
   (c) Printer   (d) Touchpad

4. Which of the following is not an output device?
   (a) Printer   (b) Monitor
   (c) Plotter   (d) Mouse

5. Joystick is used for ....
   (a) Gaming   (b) Weather forecast
   (c) Word processing (d) None of these

6. Which of the following is not an operating system?
   (a) Android   (b) Macos
   (c) Linux   (d) Samsung

7. Which one of the options is not shown in control panel?
   (a) Sound   (b) Mouse
   (c) Display   (d) My Account

8. A computer doesn't 'boot' if it doesn't have the ....
   (a) Compiler
   (b) Loader
   (c) Operating system
   (d) Assembler

9. Which of the following is built in memory of a computer ....
   (a) RAM   (b) ROM
   (c) MODEM   (d) Motherboard

10. Output which is made up of pictures, sounds and video is called ....
    (a) COM   (b) Hard copy
    (c) Graphics   (d) Multimedia

11. A compiler translates a programme written in high level language into ....
    (a) Machine language
    (b) An algorithm
    (c) Java
    (d) Binary system

12. OCR stands for ....
(a) Optical Character Recognition
(b) Optical CPU Recognition
(c) Optical Character Reading
(d) None of the above

13. Which of the following functions are not performed by servers?
(a) E-mail processing
(b) Database sharing
(c) Word processing
(d) Processing websites

14. Which of the following is not a search engine?
(a) Google
(b) Yahoo
(c) Firefox Mozila
(d) Altavista

15. Who created the C programming language?
(a) Ken Thompson
(b) Dennis Ritchie
(c) Robin Milner
(d) None of the above

16. Who is known as Father of Internet?
(a) Alan Perlis
(b) Vint Cerf
(c) Jean Sammet
(d) Steve Lawrence

17. One Terabyte (1 TB) is equal to ....
(a) 1028 GB
(b) 1012 GB
(c) 2024 GB
(d) 1024 GB

18. First computer virus was known as ....
(a) Rabbit
(b) Creeper Virus
(c) Elk Cloner
(d) SCA Virus

19. What is URL ?
(a) A computer software programme
(b) A type of UFO
(c) The address of document
(d) Software

20. What is the full form of PDF?
(a) Printed Document Format
(b) Public Document Format
(c) Portable Document Format
(d) Published Document Format

2 Marks Questions

21. Which of the following is/are true?
1. A virus is a small piece of software that harms files and program on the computer.
2. Keyboard, mouse and light pen are the input devices.

Codes
(a) Both 1 and 2
(b) Only 1
(c) Only 2
(d) All of the above

22. State T for true and F for false for the given statements.
1. A server is a computer that provides data to other computers.
2. Hard disk is made up of a metal disk and coated with a metal oxide used to store bulk of data.
3. Memory card or flash memory card is a memory device.

Codes

	A	B	C			A	B	C
(a)	T	T	T		(b)	F	T	F
(c)	T	T	F		(d)	F	F	T

23. Which of the following pair is not correctly matched?
(a) Operating System–Windows
(b) Programming Language–Fortran
(c) Primary memory–Magnetic tapes
(d) Input device-Mouse

Chapter 16

General Knowledge

1 Mark Questions

1. The first Vice-President of India is ....
   (a) Dr. Radhakrishnan
   (b) Dr. Rajendra Prasad
   (c) Dr. Zakir Hussain
   (d) Badruddin Tyabji

2. The first woman to climb Mount Everest ....
   (a) Bachendri Pal   (b) Shanno Devi
   (c) Santosh Yadav   (d) Nirja Bhanot

3. Which of the following is the first bank of India?
   (a) Reserve Bank of India
   (b) State Bank of India
   (c) Union Bank Of India
   (d) Bank Of Hindustan

4. Who is the first Indian to scored triple century in Test cricket?
   (a) Virender Sehwag
   (b) Sachin Tendulkar
   (c) Rahul Dravid
   (d) Saurav Ganguly

5. .... was the first Viceroy of India.
   (a) Lord Canning   (b) Lord Cornwallis
   (c) Lord Wellesley   (d) Lord W Bentinck

6. The First Post Office opened in India in ....
   (a) Delhi   (b) Kolkata
   (c) Mumbai   (d) Chennai

7. Who was the first President of USA?
   (a) John Adams
   (b) George Washington
   (c) Abraham Lincoln
   (d) George H W Bush

8. The highest lake of India is ....
   (a) Devtal Lake
   (b) Chandratal Lake
   (c) Wular Lake
   (d) Loktak Lake

9. The longest dam of India 'Hirakund' Dam is located in ....
   (a) Uttarakhand   (b) Odisha
   (c) Chhattisgarh   (d) Punjab

10. The state with longest coastal line is ....
    (a) Maharashtra
    (b) Tamil Nadu
    (c) Gujarat
    (d) Goa

11. Which country is known as the 'Land of Midnight Sun'?
(a) Japan
(b) Norway
(c) Canada
(d) Australia

12. .... is called as the Sugar Bowl of the world.
(a) Cuba
(b) China
(c) Denmark
(d) India

13. Which is considered as the Gift of Nile?
(a) Russia
(b) Brazil
(c) Egypt
(d) Turkey

14. .... is known as Land of White Elephant.
(a) Indonesia
(b) Thailand
(c) Mauritius
(d) Canada

15. Which city is known as city of palaces?
(a) Mumbai
(b) Kolkata
(c) New York
(d) Rome

16. Shantivan is crematorium of ....
(a) Indira Gandhi
(b) Jawaharlal Nehru
(c) Rajiv Gandhi
(d) Mahatma Gandhi

17. The crematorium of Mahatma Gandhi is located in ....
(a) Vijay Ghat
(b) Raj Ghat
(c) Veer Bhumi
(d) Shakti Sthal

2 Marks Questions

18. Which of the following statement is true?

1. United States of America has the World's largest railway network.

2. Waterways are the fastest means of communications in the world.

Codes
(a) Only 1
(b) Only 2
(c) Both 1 and 2
(d) All of these

19. Which of the following is matched correctly?

List I		List II
A. Olympics, 2008	1.	Beijing
B. Olympics, 2012	2.	London
C. Olympics, 2016	3.	Rio de Janeiro

Codes
(a) Only 1
(b) Only 1 and 2
(c) Only 2 and 3
(d) All of the above

20. Which of the following is correctly matched?

1. Highest Airport of India-Leh Airport

2. Longest railway platform of India-Gorakhpur

3. Largest lake of India-Chilika Lake

Codes
(a) Only 1
(b) Both 1 and 2
(c) Only 3
(d) All of these

21. Match List I with List II.

List I		List II
A. First Man to reach North Pole	1.	Robert Peary
B. First Man to reach South Pole	2.	Roald Amundsen
C. First space tourist	3.	Dennis Tito

Codes

	A	B	C		A	B	C
(a)	1	2	3	(b)	3	2	1
(c)	2	3	1	(d)	3	1	2

Chapter 17

Books and Authors

1 Mark Questions

1. Which among the following books is written by Munshi Premchand?
   (a) Godan
   (b) Karmbhumi
   (c) Rangbhumi
   (d) All of these

2. Which of the following books is written by Jawaharlal Nehru?
   (a) Discovery of India
   (b) Train to Pakistan
   (c) The Midnight's Children
   (d) The Hindu View of Life

3. Who has written the famous book Gulliver's Travels?
   (a) E.M Forster
   (b) Leo Tolstoy
   (c) George Orwell
   (d) Jonathan Swift

4. The book 'The Indian War of Independence' is written by ....
   (a) BG Tilak
   (b) Madam Cuma
   (c) VD Savarkar
   (d) MK Gandhi

5. Who among the following is a famous English writer?
   (a) Mahadevi Verma
   (b) Mulk Raj Anand
   (c) Munshi Premchand
   (d) Sumitranandan Pant

6. The book 'What Went Wrong and Why' is authored by ....
   (a) Kiran Bedi
   (b) Kiran Desai
   (c) Arundhati Roy
   (d) Jhumpa Lahiri

7. Who is the author of 'Cry, the Peacock'?
   (a) Anita Desai
   (b) Arundhati Roy
   (c) Kiran Desai
   (d) R K Narayan

8. The famous book 'The Daughter of the East' is written by ....
   (a) Benazir Bhutto
   (b) Taslima Nasrin
   (c) Kiran Desai
   (d) Amrita Pritam

9. .... is the author of book 'India Wins Freedom'.
   (a) Indira Gandhi
   (b) BR Ambedkar
   (c) Dr. Rajendra Prasad
   (d) Maulana Abdul Kalam Azad

10. Which of the following books is written by Jai Shankar Prasad?
    (a) Kamayani
    (b) Gaban
    (c) Yama
    (d) Urvashi

11. Harivansh Rai Bachchan is the author of ....
    (a) Madhushala
    (b) Milan Yamini
    (c) Nisha Nimantran
    (d) All of the above

12. Name the author of the book 'Wings of Fire'.
    (a) Narendra Modi
    (b) Jawaharlal Nehru
    (c) A.P.J. Abdul Kalam
    (d) None of the above

2 Marks Questions

13. Which of the following is/are true?
    1. 'Born Again on Mountain' book is written by Arunima Sinha.
    2. 'Bhagwat Gita and Mahabharat' is written by Vedvyas.

    Codes
    (a) Only 1
    (b) Only 2
    (c) Both 1 and 2
    (d) None of the above

14. Which is correctly matched?
    1. Baba Ramdev–My Life My Mission
    2. Malala Yousafzai–We Are Displaced
    3. Narendra Modi–Exam Warriors

    Codes
    (a) Only 1   (b) Both 1 and 2
    (c) Both 2 and 3   (d) All of these

15. Consider the following statements.
    1. The book 'Discovery of India' is written by Mahatma Gandhi.
    2. The book 'Ignited Minds' is written by Abdul Kalam.

    Which one of the following statement is/are correct?

    Codes
    (a) Only 1   (b) Only 2
    (c) Both 1 and 2   (d) None of these

16. Consider the following statements.
    1. 'The Diary of a young girl' book is written by Anne Frank.
    2. Sarojini Naidu is the author of the book 'Broken Wings'.
    3. 'Moonwalk' book is written by Michael Jackson.

    Which one of the following statement is/are correct?

    Codes
    (a) Only 1
    (b) Only 2
    (c) Only 3
    (d) All of the above

Chapter 18

Awards and Honours

1 Mark Questions

1. Which country awards the Nobel Prize?
   (a) Ireland (b) Sweden
   (c) England (d) America

2. Who among the following is not a recipient of Bharat Ratna?
   (a) Vinobha Bhave
   (b) Sardar Vallabhbhai Patel
   (c) Lal Bahadur Shastri
   (d) Mahatma Gandhi

3. Who was the first Indian to receive a Nobel Prize?
   (a) Mother Teresa
   (b) Hargobind Tagore
   (c) CV Raman
   (d) Rabindranath Tagore

4. Which of the following is India's highest honour in the field of literature?
   (a) Vyas Samman
   (b) Kalidas Samman
   (c) Jnanpith Award
   (d) Saraswati Samman

5. The first woman to get the Bharat Ratna Award is ....
   (a) Indira Gandhi
   (b) Mother Teresa
   (c) Sarojini Naidu
   (d) Lata Mangeshkar

6. Nobel Prize is not awarded in which of the following field?
   (a) Chemistry (b) Physics
   (c) Literature (d) Architecture

7. Who is the first non-Indian to receive the Bharat Ratna?
   (a) Mother Teresa
   (b) Zubin Metra
   (c) Martin Luther King
   (d) Khan Abdul Gaffar Khan

8. Dronacharya Award is given in the field of ....
   (a) Literature (b) Archery
   (c) Sport Coaching (d) Peace

9. Har Gobind Khorana received the Noble Prize in which of the following fields?
   (a) Physics (b) Chemistry
   (c) Literature (d) Medicine

10. Ramon Magsaysay Award is named after the former President of ....
    (a) Thailand
    (b) Philippines
    (c) Indonesia
    (d) Indian Journalist's Association

11. Oscar Awards are associated with ....
    (a) Sports (b) Music
    (c) Literature (d) Films

12. Saraswati Samman is given annually for outstanding contribution to ....
(a) Classical music   (b) Fine arts
(c) Literature   (d) Education

13. The Pulitzer Prize is associated with ....
(a) Journalism   (b) Sports
(c) Literature   (d) Bravery

14. The second-highest military honorary award in India is ....
(a) Param Vir Chakra (b) Mahavir Chakra
(c) Vir Chakra   (d) Ashok Chakra

15. The first person to be awarded with Param Vir Chakra was ....
(a) Somnath Sharma
(b) Abdul Hamid
(c) Albert Ekka
(d) Sam Manekshaw

16. Amartya Sen was honoured with Nobel Prize in the field of ....
(a) Economics
(b) Biology
(c) Literature
(d) Peace

17. Who was the first Indian to get Nobel Prize in Physics?
(a) Rabindranath Tagore
(b) CV Raman
(c) Amartya Sen
(d) A.P.J. Abdul Kalam

18. The first film personality to receive Bharat Ratna Award is ....
(a) Dada Saheb Phalke
(b) Ashok Kumar
(c) Satyajit Ray
(d) Prithviraj Kapoor

2 Marks Questions

19. Which of the following is/are true?
1. Padma Vibhushan is the second highest civilian award of India.
2. Satyendra Nath Bose was one of the first recipient of Padma Vibhushan Award.

Codes
(a) Only 1   (b) Only 2
(c) Both 1 and 2   (d) Neither 1 nor 2

20. Consider the following statements.
1. CV Raman won the Nobel Prize in the field of Physics.
2. Nobel Prize is given by Netherland.
3. Nobel Prize was not awarded between 1940-42 due to World War II.

Codes
(a) Only 1 and 3   (b) Only 2
(c) Both 2 and 3   (d) All of these

21. Match List I with List II

	List I		List II
A.	Dhyan Chand Award	1.	Poetry
B.	Jnanpith Award	2.	Physics
C.	Abel Prize	3.	Sports and Games

Codes

	A	B	C		A	B	C
(a)	3	2	1	(b)	1	2	3
(c)	2	3	1	(d)	1	3	2

22. Which of the following is not correctly matched?
(a) Vyas Samman–Hindi Literature
(b) Sahitya Akademi Awards–Literature (24 languages)
(c) Shanti Swarup Bhatnagar Prize–Science and Technology
(d) Arjuna Award-Cinema

Sports

1 Mark Questions

1. Tiger Woods associated with ....
   (a) Golf   (b) Formula 1
   (c) Polo   (d) Badminton

2. The term 'white wash' is associated with which game?
   (a) Football   (b) Hockey
   (c) Cricket   (d) Tennis

3. Cristiano Ronaldo is associated with which game?
   (a) Cricket   (b) Lawn Tennis
   (c) Football   (d) Kabaddi

4. Novak Djokovic is a ....
   (a) Finnish tennis player
   (b) Russian tennis player
   (c) Polish tennis player
   (d) Serbian tennis player

5. The 'Thomas Cup' is associated with ....
   (a) Table Tennis   (b) Badminton
   (c) Football   (d) Cricket

6. When was the Olympic Flame first introduced in the Winter Olympics?
   (a) 1904   (b) 1924   (c) 1936   (d) 1900

7. Where was the first Asian Games held?
   (a) Jakarta   (b) Kathmandu
   (c) New Delhi   (d) Islamabad

8. The 2023 Cricket World Cup is scheduled to be held in which country?
   (a) UAE   (b) Australia
   (c) India   (d) England

9. The term 'Tee' is used commonly in which among the following sports?
   (a) Tennis   (b) Polo
   (c) Golf   (d) Racing

10. In Kho-Kho, the players occupying the squares are known as ....
    (a) Lobby   (b) Raiders
    (c) Chasers   (d) Chukker

11. Who was the first tennis player to win an olympic medal from India?
    (a) Rohan Bopanna (b) Sania Mirza
    (c) Leander Paes   (d) Mahesh Bhupati

12. Durand Cup is associated with ....
    (a) Kabaddi   (b) Football
    (c) Baduriat   (d) Cricket

13. Who was the first badminton player from India to win an olympic medal?
(a) Saina Nehwal
(b) P.V. Sindhu
(c) Pullela Gopichand
(d) Prakash Padukone

14. Which country will host the 2026 Asian Games?
(a) China   (b) Japan
(c) Philippines   (d) South Korea

15. Neeraj Chopra is a famous played associated with which sports?
(a) Wrestling   (b) Javelin Throw
(c) Badminton   (d) Cricket

16. Abhinav Bindra won India's first individual Olympic gold medal in ………… .
(a) Archery   (b) Shooting
(c) Wrestling   (d) Boxing

17. Narendra Modi Stadium is related with which sport?
(a) Cricket   (b) Volleyball
(c) Badminton   (d) Tennis

18. Which among the following is a football player?
(a) Sunil Chhetri   (b) Gagan Narang
(c) Yageshwar Dutt   (d) Kuldeep Yadav

2 Marks Questions

19. Match List I with List II.

List I		List II
A. Somdev Devvarman	1.	Badminton
B. Saurabh Chaudhary	2.	Shooting
C. Anita Sood	3.	Golf
D. Saina Nehwal	4.	Tennis

Codes

	A	B	C	D
(a)	1	2	3	4
(b)	2	1	3	4
(c)	4	2	3	1
(d)	3	1	2	4

20. Which of the following is not correctly matched?
(a) Abhinav Bindra – Shooting
(b) Michael Phelps – Swimming
(c) Maria Sharapova – Tennis
(d) Kane Williamson – Boxing

21. Which of the following is correctly matched?
1. Aga Khan Cup-Football
2. Uber Cup-Golf
3. Durand Cup-Hockey

Codes
(a) Only 1   (b) Only 3
(c) Both 2 and 3   (d) All of these

22. State T for true and F for false for the given statements.
1. Davis Cup is related with Lawn Tennis.
2. Santosh Trophy is related with Football.
3. Wimbeldon Trophy is associated with Badminton.

Codes

	A	B	C			A	B	C
(a)	T	F	T		(b)	F	T	F
(c)	T	F	F		(d)	T	T	F

PRACTICE SET 01

1 Mark Questions

1. Ajatshatru belonged to which dynasty?
(a) Shishunaga dynasty
(b) Haryanka dynasty
(c) Saka dynasty
(d) Mauryan dynasty

2. Which is the first site discovered in the Indus Valley Civilisation?
(a) Lothal   (b) Kalibangan
(c) Harappa   (d) Mohenjo Daro

3. The Great emperor 'Ashoka' was inspired by the teaching of ....
(a) Bindusara   (b) Bimbisara
(c) Buddha   (d) Chandragupta

4. Which of the following composed the Tamil Epic 'Silappatikaram'?
(a) Satthanar   (b) Ilango
(c) Ved Vyasa   (d) Valmiki

5. Which among the following monuments is located in Odisha?
(a) Sun Temple
(b) Sanchi Stupa
(c) Golgumbaz
(d) Monuments of Hampi

6. The largest cricket stadium of the world is located in ....
(a) Maharashtra   (b) Gujarat
(c) Madhya Pradesh
(d) Uttar Pradesh

7. Which of the following articles deals with the President of India?
(a) Article 148   (b) Article 52
(c) Article 76   (d) Article 32

8. Article 243 is related to ....
(a) Panchayati Raj
(b) Election Commission
(c) Finance Commission
(d) Fundamental Rights

9. Part IX A of Indian Constitution deals with ....
(a) Election
(b) Municipalities
(c) Finance Commission
(d) Governor

10. Bengaluru is the headquarter of ....
(a) Defence Research and Development Organisation
(b) Indian Space Research Organisation
(c) Indian Council for Medical Research
(d) National Infrastructure Fund

11. F.G Otis was the inventor of ....
(a) Microphone   (b) Transformer
(c) Aeroplane   (d) Lift

12. Which of the following is Chemical change?
(a) Cooking of food
(b) Freezing of water
(c) Cutting of tree
(d) Breaking of stone

13. Which is world's fastest missile ship commissioned in 1997?
(a) INS Vikrant
(b) INS Viraat
(c) INS Prahar
(d) INS Karanj

14. The computer monitor is which type of device?
    (a) Input   (b) Output
    (c) Processor   (d) Software

15. The main system board of a computer is called the ....
    (a) Integrated circuit (b) Mother board
    (c) Microchip   (d) Processor

16. Dadasaheb Phalke Award is given in ...... field.
    (a) Cinema   (b) Music
    (c) Sports   (d) Politics

17. The Noble Prize is awarded by which among the following countries?
    (a) England   (b) Poland
    (c) Sweden   (d) Denmark

18. .... is responsible for depletion of Ozone.
    (a) Carbon Monoxide
    (b) Carbon Dioxide
    (c) Chlorofluoro Carbon
    (d) Oxygen

19. The headquarters of ISRO is located in ....
    (a) Ahmedabad   (b) Bengaluru
    (c) Sriharikota   (d) Chandipur

20. The first state to adopt Panchayati Raj System in India was ....
    (a) Madhya Pradesh
    (b) Haryana
    (c) Andhra Pradesh
    (d) Rajasthan

21. The hand written books a long ago were called ....
    (a) Inscription   (b) Epics
    (c) Manuscript   (d) Holy books

22. The ruler of Delhi sultanate 'Qutubuddin Aibak' was succeeded by ....
    (a) Iltutmish   (b) Razia Sultan
    (c) Alauddin Khilji   (d) Sikandar Lodhi

23. The oldest veda 'Rigveda' includes more than .... hymns.
    (a) one thousands
    (b) two thousands
    (c) three thousands
    (d) five hundred

24. The Harappa site 'Lothal' is located in which of the following states?
    (a) Haryana   (b) Punjab
    (c) Uttar Pradesh   (d) Gujarat

25. Gautam Buddha was born in ....
    (a) 463 BC   (b) 272 BC
    (c) 563 BC   (d) 361 BC

26. Nargis Dutt was the first lady actress to receive the............Award.
    (a) Bharat Ratna
    (b) Padma Shri Award
    (c) Padma Vibhushan
    (d) Padma Bhushan

27. Which among the following books is authored by Jhumpa Lahiri?
    (a) The Namesake
    (b) The God of Small Things
    (c) A Suitable Boy
    (d) Three Mistakes of My Life

28. .... was the India's first Test Captain?
    (a) Rahul Dravid   (b) Sunil Gavaskar
    (c) CK Naidu   (d) Kapil Dev

29. PV Sindhu is associated with ....
    (a) Kabaddi   (b) Archery
    (c) Badminton   (d) Cricket

30. .... longitude is considered as Indian Standard Time.

(a) $82\frac{1}{2}°E$ (b) $23\frac{1}{2}°N$

(c) $23\frac{1}{2}°S$ (d) $66\frac{1}{2}°N$

31. The book 'Cry the Peacock' is authored by ....
    (a) Arundhati Roy
    (b) Khushwant Singh
    (c) Anita Desai
    (d) Charles Dickens

32. Winter Solstice occurs on ....
    (a) 22nd December (b) 21st March
    (c) 21st June   (d) 23rd September

33. Which is the 2nd largest continent after Asia?
    (a) Asia   (b) Antarctica
    (c) Australia (d) Africa

34. The world's deepest Trench 'Mariana Trench' is located in ....
    (a) Pacific Ocean (b) Atlantic Ocean
    (c) Arctic Ocean   (d) Indian Ocean

35. Which among the following is a Volcanic mountain?
    (a) Himalyan Mountain
    (b) Aravalli Mountain
    (c) Vosges Mountain
    (d) Mt. Fujiyama

36. 'The National Girl Child Day' is observed on ....
    (a) 7th April   (b) 24th January
    (c) 24th October (d) 12th January

37. Largest fresh water lake in the world is ....
    (a) Caspian Lake (b) Lake Superior
    (c) Baikal Lake   (d) Titicaca Lake

38. India is situated in which hemisphere?
    (a) Southern (b) Eastern
    (c) Western   (d) Northern

39. Which type of forests are found in North-Eastern states?
    (a) Tropical Rain Forest
    (b) Thorny Bushes
    (c) Mangrove Forest
    (d) Tropical Deciduous Forest

40. Which among the following is the largest planet in the Solar System?
    (a) Jupiter (b) Mars
    (c) Saturn   (d) Uranus

2 Marks Questions

41. Which of the following is true?
    1. The largest state in India in terms of area is Rajasthan.
    2. The River Narmada falls in the Arabian Sea.

    Codes
    (a) Only 1   (b) Only 2
    (c) Both 1 and 2
    (d) Neither 1 nor 2

42. Which of the following is true?
    1. Most of Ashoka's inscriptions were in Prakrit and were written in the Brahmi script.
    2. Ashoka was the founder of Mauryan Dynasty.

    Codes
    (a) Only 1   (b) Only 2
    (c) Both 1 and 2 (d) Neither 1 nor 2

43. Which of the following is true?

1. The Deccan plateau of India is one of the oldest plateau.
2. Lakshadweep Islands are located in Arabian Sea.
3. The Himalyan Moutains are divided into three main parallel ranges.

Codes
(a) Ony 1   (b) Only 2
(c) Both 1 and 3   (d) All of these

44. State T for true and F for false for the given statements.

A. The sportperson Dipa Karmakar is associated with Gymnastics.
B. The book 'Wings of Fire' is authored by APJ Abdul Kalam.
C. Dudhwa National Park is located in Bihar.

Codes

	A	B	C			A	B	C
(a)	T	F	T		(b)	F	T	F
(c)	T	T	F		(d)	F	F	T

45. Which of the following is true?

1. More than 71% of the Earth is covered with water.
2. The Arctic Ocean is located within the Arctic circle and surrounds the North Pole.
3. Asia continent lies in the Eastern Hemisphere.

Codes
(a) Only 1
(b) Only 2
(c) Both 1 and 3
(d) All of the above

46. Consider the following statements.

1. In a Municipal Corporation, the elected members are called ward councillors.
2. Zila Parishad is the first tier of democratic government.
3. Panchayati Raj System is a process through which people participate in their own government.

Which of the given statements is/are true?
(a) Only 1   (b) Both 2 and 3
(c) Only 3   (d) All of these

47. Which is correctly matched?

1. Gir National Park-Gujarat
2. Pench National Park-Uttar Pradesh
3. Sundarbans National Park-West Bengal

Codes
(a) Only 1   (b) Both 2 and 3
(c) Both 1 and 3   (d) All of these

48. Match the following.

	Mahajanpadas		Capitals
A.	First man travel in space	1.	George Washington
B.	First man to fly an aeroplane	2.	Neil Armstrong
C.	First man to set foot on moon	3.	Wright Brothers
D.	First President of USA	4.	Yuri Gagarin

Codes

	A	B	C	D			A	B	C	D
(a)	2	4	3	1		(b)	4	2	1	3
(c)	1	4	3	2		(d)	4	3	2	1

49. Match the following.

	Monuments		Places
A.	Ajanta Caves	1.	Aurangabad
B.	Lotus Temple	2.	Delhi
C.	Amer Fort	3.	Jaipur

Codes

	A	B	C
(a)	1	2	3
(b)	3	2	1
(c)	2	1	3
(d)	2	3	1

50. Match the following.

	Rulers		Dynasty
A.	Bimbisara	1.	Gupta Dynasty
B.	Samudra Gupta	2.	Haryanka Dynasty
C.	Kanishka	3.	Satavahana Dynasty
D.	Gautamiputra Satakarni	4.	Kushan Dynasty

Codes

	A	B	C	D		A	B	C	D
(a)	1	2	3	4	(b)	2	1	4	3
(c)	4	3	2	1	(d)	3	4	1	2

PRACTICE SET 

1 Mark Questions

1. In which Buddhist Council, Buddhism was divided into Mahayana and Hinayana sects?
(a) First Buddhist Council
(b) Second Buddhist Council
(c) Third Buddhist Council
(d) Fourth Buddhist Council

2. The great bath of Indus Valley Civilisation is found at ....
(a) Kalibangan   (b) Mohenjo Daro
(c) Lothal   (d) Dholavira

3. Who among the following known as the 'slave of a slave'?
(a) Muhammad bin Qasim
(b) Mahmud of Ghazni
(c) Iltutmish   (d) Qutubuddin Aibak

4. Painting reached its highest level of development during the reign of ....
(a) Akbar   (b) Aurangzeb
(c) Jahangir   (d) Shah Jahan

5. Which caves are well known for their Indian-rock cut architecture?
(a) Khajuraho   (b) Hampi
(c) Ajanta   (d) Ellora

6. Which heritage site is famous for its Chalukya style of architecture?
(a) Buland Darwaza   (b) Rani Ki Vav
(c) Pattadakal   (d) Sun Temple

7. The majority of asteroids are found between the orbits of ....
(a) Mars and Jupiter   (b) Earth and Mars
(c) Jupiter and Saturn
(d) Saturn and Uranus

8. The following planet takes maximum time for one spin on its axis ....
(a) Venus   (b) Mercury
(c) Saturn   (d) Uranus

9. The distance between the Longitudes decreases towards ....
(a) Poles   (b) Equator
(c) Tropic of Capricorn   (d) Tropic of Cancer

10. Which among the following divides the Earth into Eastern and Western part?
(a) Tropic of Cancer
(b) Tropic of Capricorn
(c) Prime Meridian   (d) Axis of the Earth

11. The highest peak in the Eastern Ghats is
(a) Anaimudi   (b) Doda Betta
(c) Ooty   (d) Jindhagada Peak

12. Which of the following divisions of India has the oldest landmass?
(a) The Himalayas
(b) The Northern Plains
(c) The Peninsular Plateau
(d) The Indian Desert

13. The trees that do not shed their leaves are mostly found in ....
(a) hot desert vegetation
(b) tropical monsoon forests
(c) coniferous forests
(d) temperate deciduous forests

14. Which of the following months has been associated with 'retreating monsoon' in India?
(a) July   (b) October
(c) April   (d) December

15. The working principle of a washing machine is ....
    (a) Centrifugation   (b) Reverse osmois
    (c) Momentum   (d) Centripeatal

16. The speed of light will be minimum while passing through ....
    (a) water (b) vacuum (c) glass   (d) air

17. Hydrogen bomb is based on the principle of ....
    (a) Nuclear fission   (b) Nuclear fusion
    (c) Natural radioactivity
    (d) Artificial radioactivity

18. Brass gets discoloured in air because of the presence of which of the following gases in air?
    (a) Hydrogen Sulphide (b) Oxygen
    (c) Nitrogen   (d) Carbon Dioxide

19. Which of the following is a viral disease?
    (a) Diphtheria   (b) Filariasis
    (c) Leprosy   (d) Influenza

20. Bioenergy is obtained from ....
    (a) Sun   (b) Coal
    (c) Biomass   (d) Petroleum

21. Africa is the world's .... largest continent.
    (a) second   (b) third
    (c) fourth   (d) None of these

22. Which of the following ranges separates Asia from Europe?
    (a) Rockies mountatins
    (b) Ural mountains
    (c) Alps mountatins (d) Andes mountains

23. Which of the following requires maximum energy?
    (a) Secondary consumer
    (b) Decomposer
    (c) Primary consumer
    (d) Primary producer

24. The upper part of an aquatic ecosystem contains ....
    (a) Nekton   (b) Plankton
    (c) Benthos   (d) Both (a) and (b)

25. Lichens are good bio-indicators for ....
    (a) environmental radiation
    (b) soil pollution
    (c) water and air pollution
    (d) None of the above

26. Who presented objective resolution on 22nd January, 1947?
    (a) B.R. Ambedkar   (b) Jawaharlal Nehru
    (c) Rajendra Prasad (d) None of these

27. The idea of 'concurrent list' in the Indian Constitution is taken from the Constitution of ....
    (a) Ireland   (b) Canada
    (c) Australia   (d) Japan

28. What is the tenure of the elected members of Rajya Sabha?
    (a) 2 years   (b) 4 years
    (c) 6 years   (d) 5 years

29. Who among the following is the presiding officer of the Lok Sabha?
    (a) President   (b) Vice-President
    (c) Speaker of Lok Sabha
    (d) Prime Minister

30. The functions of Panchayati Raj is provided in which Schedule of Constitution of India?
    (a) Eighth Schedule
    (b) Ninth Schedule
    (c) Seventh Schedule
    (d) Eleventh Schedule

31. The idea of the Constitution of India was flashed for the first time by ....
    (a) M.N. Roy   (b) B.R. Ambedkar
    (c) Jawaharlal Nehru (d) None of these

32. .... is the process of dividing the disk into tracks and sector.
    (a) Tracking　　(b) Formatting
    (c) Crashing　　(d) Allotting

33. You can change settings of your computer by ....
    (a) My document　　(b) Control panel
    (c) Files　　(d) None of these

34. First Woman President of UN General Assembly was ....
    (a) Indira Gandhi　　(b) Sarojini Naidu
    (c) Vijya Lakshmi Pandit
    (d) Margaret Thatcher

35. First Indian Woman to win a medal in Wrestling is ....
    (a) Sakshi Malik　　(b) PV Sindhu
    (c) Navjot Kaur　　(d) Babita Phogat

36. The first woman to receive Ashoka Chakra was ....
    (a) Neerja Bhanot　　(b) Santosh Yadav
    (c) Shanno Devi　　(d) Harita Kaur Dayal

37. .... is the oldest and the highest Indian literary award.
    (a) Jnanpith Award
    (b) Sahitya Akademi Award
    (c) Vyas Samman
    (d) Saraswati Samman

38. Which of the following books is not written by Munshi Premchand?
    (a) Gaban　　(b) Godan
    (c) Panchtantra　　(d) Nirmla

39. Harmanpreet Kaur is associated with ....
    (a) Hockey　　(b) Kabaddi
    (c) Cricket　　(d) Kho kho

40. The largest Football stadium in India is ....
    (a) Narendra Modi Stadium
    (b) Salt lake Stadium
    (c) Keenan Stadium
    (d) Eden Gardens

2 Marks Questions

41. Which of the following statements is/are true?
    1. The first Common Wealth Games were held in Hamilton in 1930.
    2. The first Cricket World Cup was organised in England in 1975.
    Codes
    (a) Only 1　　(b) Only 2
    (c) Both 1 and 2　　(d) Neither 1 nor 2

42. Which of the following pairs is not correctly matched?
    (a) Kaziranga National Park-Assam
    (b) Buxa Tiger Reserve-Uttar Pradesh
    (c) Hemis National Park-Ladakh
    (d) Kanha National Park-Madhya Pradesh

43. Which of the following statements is/are true?
    1. The houses of Indus Valley Civilisation were made up of burnt bricks.
    2. Rigveda is the oldest text in the world.
    3. Ashoka was the son of Bindusara.
    Codes
    (a) Only 1　　(b) Only 2
    (c) Both 1 and 3　　(d) All of these

44. Consider the following statements.

1. The Constituent Assembly was formed in November 1946.
2. Steering Committee was headed by BR Ambedkar.
3. The Indian Constitution is lengthiest in the world.

Which of the given statements is/are true?

(a) Only 1 (b) Only 2
(c) Both 1 and 3 (d) All of these

45. State T for true and F for false for the given statements.

1. Africa is the only continent which is intersected by Tropic of Cancer, Equator and Tropic of Capricorn.
2. Pampas is the most fertile region of South America.
3. India is the 7th largest country in the world (in terms of area).

Codes

(a) Only 1 (b) Only 2
(c) Both 1 and 2 (d) All of these

46. Which is correctly matched?

1. Fold Mountains – Rockies
2. Block Mountains – Satpura
3. Volcanic Mountains – Cotapaxi

Codes

(a) Only 1 (b) Only 2
(c) Both 1 and 3 (d) All of these

47. State T for true and F for false for the given statements.

A. The first country to appoint Lokpal is Sweden.
B. USA is the first country to make written Constitution.
C. Marco Polo was the first European to visit China.

Codes

	A	B	C		A	B	C
(a)	T	F	T	(b)	F	T	T
(c)	F	T	F	(d)	T	T	T

48. Which of the following is correctly matched?

Sport Personalities		Associated with
1. Manpreet Singh	–	Hockey
2. Dutee Chand	–	Athletics
3. Hima Das	–	Archery

Codes

(a) Only 1 (b) Only 2
(c) Both 1 and 2 (d) All of these

49. Match the following.

	List I	List II
A.	North-South Extent of India	1. 3200 km
B.	East-West Extent of India	2. 2900 km
C.	Total coastal line of India	3. 7516 km

Codes

	A	B	C		A	B	C
(a)	1	2	3	(b)	3	2	1
(c)	2	1	3	(d)	1	3	2

50. Match the following.

	List I	List II
A.	Panchtantra	1. Vishnu Sharma
B.	The Namesake	2. Jhumpa Lahiri
C.	The Discovery of India	3. Pt. JL Nehru
D.	Life Divine	4. Aurobindo Ghosh

Codes

	A	B	C	D		A	B	C	D
(a)	1	2	3	4	(b)	4	3	2	1
(c)	3	4	1	2	(d)	2	1	4	3

Answers

Chapter 1   Ancient History of India

1. (c)	2. (d)	3. (b)	4. (a)	5. (a)	6. (d)	7. (a)	8. (a)	9. (a)	10. (c)
11. (b)	12. (b)	13. (d)	14. (c)	15. (b)	16. (b)	17. (a)	18. (b)	19. (a)	20. (d)
21. (a)	22. (b)	23. (b)	24. (b)	25. (b)	26. (a)	27. (a)	28. (a)	29. (c)	30. (a)

Chapter 2   Famous Rulers and Kingdoms

1. (a)	2. (a)	3. (a)	4. (b)	5. (c)	6. (b)	7. (a)	8. (a)	9. (a)	10. (a)
11. (b)	12. (d)	13. (b)	14. (d)	15. (a)	16. (b)	17. (b)	18. (a)	19. (d)	20. (b)
21. (d)	22. (c)	23. (c)	24. (b)	25. (c)	26. (a)	27. (a)	28. (d)		

Chapter 3   Historical Monuments, Art and Architecture

1. (b)	2. (c)	3. (a)	4. (d)	5. (a)	6. (a)	7. (a)	8. (a)	9. (c)	10. (b)
11. (b)	12. (a)	13. (b)	14. (a)	15. (a)	16. (a)	17. (b)	18. (a)	19. (a)	20. (a)
21. (b)	22. (a)	23. (c)	24. (c)	25. (b)	26. (c)	27. (c)	28. (b)		

Chapter 4   Solar System

1. (a)	2. (c)	3. (d)	4. (b)	5. (d)	6. (a)	7. (a)	8. (a)	9. (b)	10. (b)
11. (c)	12. (b)	13. (a)	14. (c)	15. (d)	16. (b)	17. (a)	18. (d)	19. (b)	20. (d)
21. (c)	22. (b)	23. (c)	24. (c)	25. (a)	26. (a)	27. (c)	28. (c)	29. (a)	30. (c)
31. (d)	32. (a)								

Chapter 5   Our Earth

1. (b)	2. (a)	3. (a)	4. (b)	5. (a)	6. (a)	7. (d)	8. (c)	9. (a)	10. (a)
11. (b)	12. (a)	13. (c)	14. (a)	15. (b)	16. (b)	17. (b)	18. (a)	19. (a)	20. (b)
21. (a)	22. (d)	23. (c)	24. (c)	25. (b)					

Chapter 6   Continents and Oceans

1. (c)	2. (b)	3. (c)	4. (a)	5. (c)	6. (a)	7. (b)	8. (a)	9. (a)	10. (c)
11. (a)	12. (a)	13. (b)	14. (b)	15. (a)	16. (b)	17. (a)	18. (c)	19. (a)	20. (a)
21. (b)	22. (a)	23. (c)	24. (c)	25. (a)	26. (a)				

Chapter 7   Our Country-Location and Physical Division

1. (a)	2. (b)	3. (a)	4. (b)	5. (b)	6. (c)	7. (a)	8. (d)	9. (b)	10. (c)
11. (c)	12. (a)	13. (a)	14. (a)	15. (a)	16. (d)	17. (a)	18. (a)	19. (a)	20. (b)
21. (b)	22. (c)	23. (a)	24. (d)	25. (b)	26. (c)	27. (b)	28. (c)	29. (a)	30. (c)
31. (b)	32. (c)	33. (d)	34. (a)						

1. (a)	**2.** (b)	**3.** (c)	**4.** (a)	**5.** (b)	**6.** (c)	**7.** (d)	**8.** (d)	**9.** (b)	**10.** (b)
11. (b)	**12.** (a)	**13.** (a)	**14.** (b)	**15.** (c)	**16.** (a)	**17.** (c)	**18.** (a)	**19.** (c)	**20.** (c)
21. (a)	**22.** (a)	**23.** (d)	**24.** (c)	**25.** (d)	**26.** (d)	**27.** (b)	**28.** (a)	**29.** (c)	**30.** (d)
31. (c)	**32.** (d)	**33.** (c)	**34.** (c)	**35.** (d)					

Chapter 9   Climate and Vegetation

1. (a)	**2.** (a)	**3.** (b)	**4.** (b)	**5.** (d)	**6.** (a)	**7.** (c)	**8.** (c)	**9.** (a)	**10.** (a)
11. (a)	**12.** (d)	**13.** (c)	**14.** (b)	**15.** (c)	**16.** (b)	**17.** (a)	**18.** (c)	**19.** (c)	**20.** (c)
21. (d)	**22.** (a)								

Chapter 10   Ecology and Environment

1. (c)	**2.** (a)	**3.** (d)	**4.** (d)	**5.** (b)	**6.** (c)	**7.** (d)	**8.** (a)	**9.** (b)	**10.** (b)
11. (a)	**12.** (a)	**13.** (a)	**14.** (c)	**15.** (c)	**16.** (a)	**17.** (a)	**18.** (b)	**19.** (a)	**20.** (b)
21. (b)	**22.** (b)	**23.** (a)	**24.** (a)	**25.** (c)	**26.** (d)	**27.** (c)	**28.** (b)	**29.** (c)	**30.** (a)

Chapter 11   Indian Constitution

1. (b)	**2.** (d)	**3.** (c)	**4.** (a)	**5.** (a)	**6.** (b)	**7.** (a)	**8.** (d)	**9.** (b)	**10.** (d)
11. (c)	**12.** (d)	**13.** (b)	**14.** (a)	**15.** (d)	**16.** (a)	**17.** (a)	**18.** (a)	**19.** (c)	**20.** (a)
21. (c)	**22.** (c)	**23.** (a)	**24.** (a)	**25.** (d)	**26.** (d)	**27.** (b)	**28.** (c)	**29.** (d)	**30.** (a)
31. (d)	**32.** (c)								

Chapter 12   Our Government

1. (d)	**2.** (b)	**3.** (b)	**4.** (c)	**5.** (c)	**6.** (c)	**7.** (b)	**8.** (b)	**9.** (b)	**10.** (c)
11. (b)	**12.** (c)	**13.** (b)	**14.** (c)	**15.** (b)	**16.** (b)	**17.** (a)	**18.** (a)	**19.** (a)	**20.** (b)
21. (a)	**22.** (b)	**23.** (d)	**24.** (b)	**25.** (c)	**26.** (c)	**27.** (a)	**28.** (d)	**29.** (d)	

Chapter 13   Local Government and Administration

1. (b)	**2.** (d)	**3.** (d)	**4.** (d)	**5.** (a)	**6.** (a)	**7.** (d)	**8.** (c)	**9.** (c)	**10.** (c)
11. (c)	**12.** (a)	**13.** (c)	**14.** (d)	**15.** (d)	**16.** (d)	**17.** (a)	**18.** (d)	**19.** (c)	**20.** (c)
21. (c)	**22.** (d)	**23.** (a)	**24.** (c)						

Chapter 14   Science and Technology

1. (a)	**2.** (c)	**3.** (b)	**4.** (a)	**5.** (a)	**6.** (b)	**7.** (b)	**8.** (a)	**9.** (b)	**10.** (d)
11. (b)	**12.** (b)	**13.** (a)	**14.** (c)	**15.** (a)	**16.** (a)	**17.** (d)	**18.** (c)	**19.** (b)	**20.** (b)
21. (b)	**22.** (b)	**23.** (c)	**24.** (b)	**25.** (c)	**26.** (c)	**27.** (c)	**28.** (a)	**29.** (c)	**30.** (c)
31. (c)	**32.** (b)	**33.** (c)	**34.** (d)						

Chapter 15 Computers

1. (a)	**2.** (a)	**3.** (c)	**4.** (d)	**5.** (a)	**6.** (d)	**7.** (d)	**8.** (c)	**9.** (b)	**10.** (d)
11. (a)	**12.** (a)	**13.** (c)	**14.** (d)	**15.** (b)	**16.** (b)	**17.** (d)	**18.** (b)	**19.** (c)	**20.** (c)
21. (a)	**22.** (a)	**23.** (c)							

Chapter 16 General Knowledge

1. (a)	**2.** (a)	**3.** (d)	**4.** (a)	**5.** (a)	**6.** (b)	**7.** (b)	**8.** (a)	**9.** (b)	**10.** (c)
11. (b)	**12.** (a)	**13.** (c)	**14.** (b)	**15.** (b)	**16.** (b)	**17.** (b)	**18.** (a)	**19.** (d)	**20.** (d)
21. (d)	**22.** (d)	**23.** (a)	**24.** (d)	**25.** (a)	**26.** (b)				

Chapter 17 Books and Authors

1. (d)	**2.** (a)	**3.** (d)	**4.** (c)	**5.** (b)	**6.** (a)	**7.** (a)	**8.** (a)	**9.** (d)	**10.** (a)
11. (d)	**12.** (c)	**13.** (c)	**14.** (d)	**15.** (c)	**16.** (d)				

Chapter 18 Awards and Honours

1. (b)	**2.** (d)	**3.** (d)	**4.** (c)	**5.** (a)	**6.** (d)	**7.** (d)	**8.** (c)	**9.** (d)	**10.** (b)
11. (d)	**12.** (c)	**13.** (a)	**14.** (b)	**15.** (a)	**16.** (a)	**17.** (b)	**18.** (c)	**19.** (c)	**20.** (a)
21. (a)	**22.** (d)								

Chapter 19 Sports

1. (a)	**2.** (c)	**3.** (c)	**4.** (d)	**5.** (b)	**6.** (c)	**7.** (c)	**8.** (c)	**9.** (c)	**10.** (c)
11. (c)	**12.** (b)	**13.** (b)	**14.** (b)	**15.** (b)	**16.** (b)	**17.** (a)	**18.** (a)	**19.** (c)	**20.** (d)
21. (a)	**22.** (d)								

Practice Set 1

1. (b)	**2.** (c)	**3.** (c)	**4.** (b)	**5.** (a)	**6.** (b)	**7.** (b)	**8.** (a)	**9.** (b)	**10.** (b)
11. (d)	**12.** (a)	**13.** (c)	**14.** (b)	**15.** (b)	**16.** (a)	**17.** (c)	**18.** (c)	**19.** (b)	**20.** (d)
21. (c)	**22.** (a)	**23.** (a)	**24.** (d)	**25.** (c)	**26.** (b)	**27.** (a)	**28.** (c)	**29.** (c)	**30.** (a)
31. (c)	**32.** (a)	**33.** (d)	**34.** (a)	**35.** (d)	**36.** (b)	**37.** (b)	**38.** (d)	**39.** (a)	**40.** (a)
41. (c)	**42.** (a)	**43.** (d)	**44.** (c)	**45.** (d)	**46.** (d)	**47.** (c)	**48.** (d)	**49.** (a)	**50.** (b)

Practice Set 2

1. (d)	**2.** (b)	**3.** (c)	**4.** (c)	**5.** (d)	**6.** (c)	**7.** (a)	**8.** (b)	**9.** (a)	**10.** (c)
11. (d)	**12.** (c)	**13.** (c)	**14.** (b)	**15.** (a)	**16.** (c)	**17.** (b)	**18.** (a)	**19.** (d)	**20.** (c)
21. (a)	**22.** (b)	**23.** (d)	**24.** (b)	**25.** (c)	**26.** (b)	**27.** (c)	**28.** (c)	**29.** (c)	**30.** (d)
31. (a)	**32.** (b)	**33.** (b)	**34.** (c)	**35.** (a)	**36.** (a)	**37.** (a)	**38.** (c)	**39.** (c)	**40.** (b)
41. (c)	**42.** (b)	**43.** (d)	**44.** (c)	**45.** (d)	**46.** (d)	**47.** (d)	**48.** (c)	**49.** (a)	**50.** (a)

www.ingramcontent.com/pod-product-compliance
Lightning Source LLC
LaVergne TN
LVHW080445200726
843507LV00004B/941